Rediscovering Reverence

The Path to Intimacy

OTHER BOOKS BY MATT RAWLINS

The Question
The Namer
The Container
Mysteries Beyond the Gate &
other peculiar short stories

LEADERSHIP BOOKS
The Green Bench
A dialogue about Change

The Green Bench II
Ongoing dialogue about communication

Emails from Hell

The Lottery
A question can change a life

Rediscovering Reverence

The Path to Intimacy

Matt Rawlins

Amuzement Publications

Cover by Delvyn Hunter

Rediscovering Reverence: The path to intimacy
by Matt Rawlins.

Acknowledgment

A huge 'thank you' to a brilliant writer and friend Jennifer Yeh. She was a great help in adding beauty and life to this book. Also, Tim Beals, who pushed me to put my thoughts down and organize them for a manuscript.

Table of Contents

Chapter One

The Fear of the Lord and Destiny

I have often viewed, with a dose of envious admiration, those people who claim to have "found" their destiny. What they have discerned their calling to be does not pique my interest, rather, it is their assured manner that spurs me on the quest to find my own destiny. I see something in them that I want.

I want to find the destiny that perfectly fits my life, much like a glove that will snugly fit my hand. Could there be a destiny that is perfectly tailored, intricately detailed, and lovingly fashioned by the God of the universe just for me? Something inside of me believes that God has personal destinies for each of us. There is a place where my gifts can be appreciated, my desires met, and most importantly, where He is pleased and honored by my life. Perhaps you are similar to me in that you do not know your destiny. And if you suppose you do, I want to encourage you to consider the possibility that God has much more in store for you, beyond what you can comprehend or imagine. In my case, I was astounded with what God had in store for my destiny.

Shortly after attending two years of college, I joined Youth With A Mission (YWAM) and became involved in missions within the Asia-Pacific region for almost ten years. My wife, Celia, and I then returned to my hometown in Oregon, USA, where I felt God's call to complete my Bachelor's degree. I reluctantly finished my undergraduate degree, discovered that I had a love for learning, and, unexpectedly, found myself in the quaint town of Oxford, England, pursuing a doctorate degree. I remember pushing open the heavy double doors of Oxford University Library, and walking gingerly through a room that was older than the United States. Rows of wooden shelves filled with dusty manuscripts, leather books lined the walls, mirrored rows of diligent students immersed in their studies. I would stare at the men and women engrossed in a cerebral journey of joy and pain, and wonder what issues they were pondering. These were the would-be world changers, and I felt insignificant compared to them. I spent hundreds of hours in this library, working with ideas and struggling to understand and draw conclusive results from various conduits of information. As I walked the two kilometers home, past the pub where C.S. Lewis and J.R.R. Tolkien aired their literary discussions, I would grapple with my own ideas that were at once forming and then unforming, at once shadowy and then concrete, at once appearing and then disappearing. Although the ideas were complex, I fully enjoyed the strain it placed on my mental faculties. On one of these walks, I was struck by a simple, but astounding, revelation: this is my destiny. I was—I realized—made for this particular time, to reside at this particular place, and to be studying this particular issue. *I was presently living out my destiny!* It is no wonder I took such pleasure in my studies though it was rife with difficult challenges.

God's plan for my life has been beyond the stretches of my imagination; I certainly never thought I would pursue my doctorate at Oxford Center for Missions and receive my Ph.D. through the University of Wales. When I was a very young boy, I scored borderline "mentally challenged" on an I.Q. test. If I had allowed myself to believe that assessment, my life would have amounted to mediocrity and discontentment, at best. I cringe to think the path I would have taken had God not grabbed a hold of my life; I am so thankful He did.

God had a grand plan in store for me. And in the same way He has designed great things for my life, our impartial God has also designed them for yours. The choice lies with you: will you believe that God's destiny is the best option awaiting you or will you choose to live within the limited expectations that are imposed on you by the world? Surely we can trust God and know that His plan is the best option by reading the testimonies of those who have gone before us. Through their stories, we can glean information and learn what possibilities we have for God to release our destinies.

Let us begin with Abraham. God specifically told Abraham that his life would consist of more than a simple nomadic existence. In fact, God planned to use Abraham to bless the nations of the world. Abraham's destiny was to reside within his beautiful wife Sarah. She was to give birth to a child who would be multiplied into a nation, and they would possess a bountiful land of milk and honey.

Although both Abraham and Sarah were old—and she appeared beyond the biological age of conception—Abraham accepted God's promise by faith and began to travel towards the Promised Land. When he passed through the land of Negev, Abraham's fear for King Gerar grew because he knew that the King would desire his beautiful wife. When the King came to ask him about Sarah, in deception and fear, Abraham responded that Sarah "is my sister,"[1] and gave her to him.

God intervenes at this point and orders the King to return Sarah to Abraham. When the King asked Abraham why he lied about Sarah being his wife, Abraham replied, "Because I thought, surely there is no fear of God in this place; and they will kill me because of my wife."[2]

Abraham's fear of man (i.e. King Gerar) over-
came his faith in God. The implications of
Abraham letting the King have Sarah are more
than a display of his cowardice and disobedience. By giving her away, he was also giving
away the destiny that God had specifically
promised would be birthed through Sarah.
Thankfully God was faithful even when Abraham was fearful. God was not limited to
Abraham's actions and attitude to accomplish
His work. But Abraham would eventually
learn that his destiny is linked to the fear of
God.

We will return to Abraham at a later stage. Let
us look at other men of great destinies within
the Bible. God instructed Noah to build an ark,
a simple order of huge proportions. Building
an ark that would require a hundred years of
work would take patience and perseverance;
building an ark when there was no occasion
of flooding, would take a great man of faith.
Noah was stepping out in one of the greatest visions of all time. What sustained him
through this time of testing?

"By faith Noah, being warned by God about
things not yet seen, in reverence prepared
an ark for the salvation of his household, by
which he condemned the world, and became
an heir of the righteousness which is according
to faith."[3]

It was the fear of God upon Noah's life that opened the door to his steadfast faith in the Lord and the eventual release of his destiny. All acts of obedience are born out of a reverence for God. As we have seen, and as we will further learn, destiny is only reached through obedience.

David, a young shepherd, found himself shuttling food back and forth for his brothers who were stationed in the front line of battle. During one particular food delivery, he found all of the armies of Israel, frozen in terror and hiding within their camps. They were all terrified of the giant Philistine, Goliath. For forty days, Goliath had mocked Israel and challenged an Israelite to fight him. Although all the Israelites were frightened of Goliath's size, when David saw him he bravely questioned, "For who is this uncircumcised Philistine, that he should taunt the armies of the living God?"[4]

We all know the story's conclusion. David courageously takes on the giant in the Lord's name and conquers the Philistine. But we must take note of the words David spoke as he went out to confront the giant: "You come to me with a sword, a spear, and a javelin, but I come to you in the name of the Lord of hosts, the God of the armies of Israel, whom you have taunted."[5]

David understood God's greatness and rendered Him reverence. Through a perspective of the fear of the Lord, this young man of large faith knew that he could defeat the giant with God's help. His faith was based on a thorough understanding and belief of God's greatness, and it moved him to risk his life for God's honor.

One whole generation of Jews was lost and wandering in the desert because they refused to fear God. They sent in twelve spies to search out the land and ten of them returned with a negative report: "There are giants in the land!" Only Caleb and Joshua saw the land through God's eyes, but no one would listen to them. The Israelites' lack of reverence for God cost them their inheritance and consequently, they perished in the desert. A whole generation was lost because of a lack of the fear of God.

Let's revisit Abraham. Did he eventually learn to fear God? Yes, he did. And in return, God gave Abraham a son according to His promise. When his son, Isaac, was older, God asked Abraham to offer the boy as a sacrifice. Twice before, Abraham had willingly given up Sarah because he did not fear God. Would he pass the test this time?

I put myself in Abraham's shoes. I would have argued with God. At the very least I would have stalled and prayed and asked God to reconsider His request. But Abraham immediately obeyed God's request, an indication of how much he had learned about the importance of fearing the Lord. Early the next morning, Abraham took his son to the mountains. When he finished building the altar, he tied up his son, and just as he was raising his knife, an angel intervened and said, "Do not stretch out your hand against the lad, and do nothing to him; for now I know that you fear God, since you have not withheld your son, your only Son, from Me."[6]

Somewhere along the way, Abraham learned a key lesson. He understood that his inheritance was solely based on the fear of the Lord. Hebrews 11:19 says, "He [Abraham] considered that God is able to raise men even from the dead." Abraham's reverence for God enabled him to pass the most difficult test a father could face. He reasoned that God, the author of life, would be able to raise Isaac up from the dead if He chose to. There is no reason why he shouldn't obey God. In fact, there is every reason to obey Him because He is God.

Fear of the Lord Explained

But before we continue, let us define what is this "fear" in the context of fearing the Lord. All of us experience feelings of fear. Even something as vague and intangible as the "sudden fear"[7] of the night is familiar to our minds.

Whether it's the fear of failure, the fear of stage fright, or the fear of a gaping, bleeding gunshot wound, all these fears are a result of living in a fallen world. God is love, and as John writes, "there is no fear in love, but perfect love casts out all fear."[8] Therefore if we are fearful, then we fall short of understanding the perfect love that is God—"the one who fears is not perfected in love."[9] There is one type of fear, however, that would still exist was there no sin manifest. This would be the fear of the Lord.

The German philosopher, Immanuel Kant, describes this fear as a response towards something that is sublime:

"[the sublime has] that greatness in size and degree which arouses reverence. It invites us to approach it…but it deters (for instance, the thunder above our head, or mountains towering and savage) by causing us to fear that in comparison with it we are like nothing in our own estimation."[10]

This is the type of fear that is inherent in fearing the Lord. We are invited to approach the Sublime, that is, the Lord, because He is Love. But at the same time, we fear approaching Him because we are blatantly aware of our unworthiness, our ephemeral status, and our fragile flesh. Our fear of the Lord is the tantamount to our reverence towards Him, our fear indicates awe, wonder, amazement, and it is an attitude

of veneration. Fear is the only appropriate response to His endless beauty and overarching
greatness.

Professor J. Gresham Machen of both Princeton and Westminster Theological Seminary
describes it as such: "Even the Christian must
fear God. But it is another kind of fear. It is
a fear rather of what might have been than of
what is; it is a fear of what would come were
we not in Christ. Without such fear there can
be no true love; for love of the Savior is propor-
tioned to one's horror of that from which man
has been saved."

Again, let me stress the differentiation of a
'healthy' fear of the Lord from the "fight or
flight" type of fear. The latter type of fear is an
animal instinct. God has given us the capacity
to sense danger and darkness. When we intui-
tively feel something out of the ordinary and
uncomfortable approaching us, or manifesting
within us, our bodies will automatically react
by fighting or taking flight. This physical capacity is an important physical defense mechanism and acts as an important buffer protec-
tion. Sometimes this fear also arises from an
inadequacy of our trust in God, for example,
when we fear failure, embarrassment, and re-
jection. Our physical defense mechanism also
serves as an emotional buffer, and in the same
way, we fight or take flight. Again, Profes-

sor Machen describes the delicate distinction insightfully. In the quote below, he refers to the Bible passage found in Matthew 10:28: "And fear not them which kill the body, but are not able to kill the soul; but rather fear him, which is able to destroy both soul and body in hell."

"I think, my friends that it depends altogether upon that which one is afraid. The words of our text, with the solemn inculcation of fear, are also a ringing denunciation of fear: the "Fear him" is balanced by "Fear not." The fear of God is here made a way of overcoming the fear of man. And the heroic centuries of Christian history have provided abundant testimony to it efficaciousness. With the fear of God before their eyes, the heroes of faith have boldly stood before kings and governors and said, 'Here I stand, I cannot do otherwise, God help me, Amen.'"

It is detrimental when we apply "fight or flight" fear towards God. Because many Christians have not made the clear distinction of "fear" in their minds, we sense and treat God like an ever pursuing, whip wielding nemesis. God, we fear, is ready to lash us for every sin, and His omniscience and holiness is such that, we fear, every mistake is tallied in heaven's scoreboard. This is not the case. There is little reverence inherent in this fear, it is only fear. Socrates wrote, "where there is reverence there is fear, but there is not reverence everywhere that there is fear, because fear presumably has a wider extension than reverence." Non-reverential fear—the type of fear that is not directed towards the Sublime—disables people from fearing God *out of love*. Indeed, the ingredient of reverential fear is love, and our love will direct us towards fearing, and loving, God more. Fear of the Lord produces love for the Father, and the love of the Father produces more reverence (or fear) of the Lord. This is a mutual enhancing, symbiotic relationship, it is like the never ending chicken and egg question.

So why is it difficult to understand the conception of fear and reverence? John Updike, the famous American author, believes it is because we have demystified the mystic, and attempted to explain and rationalize what cannot be made tangible:

"Our brains are no longer conditioned for reverence and awe. We cannot imagine a Second Coming that would not be cut down to size by the televised evening news, or a Last Judgment not subject to pages of holier-than-Thou second-guessing in The New York Review of Books."[11]

I agree with Updike. Our modern day society believes that the tangible is the only truth, and the supernatural realm is neglected, becoming a playground left for mediums, exorcists, and the New Age movement. There is no God in this playground, only kindergarten politics; and a holy God cannot exist amongst the arena of wrangling, cheating, duplicity, and hyperbole. Nietzsche said that if we cannot find greatness in God, than we will either deny it or create it. Sadly we have done both. Either we adamantly deny the existence of a great God and call ourselves fatalists and existentialists, or we create a religion of greatness within human institutions by worshipping our movie stars and royal monarchies.

The reverence that has been plundered from God, and applied to undeserving mortals, must be redeemed for His glory. "The essence of greatness is the perception that virtue is enough,"[12] said Emerson. Virtue is important, I concur, but God's greatness extends far beyond mere virtue. It encompasses *all* of the cardinal virtues, the universe, and the metaphysical—and that is why He commands our fear and reverence.

What is Your Destiny?

The Lord is longing to give us the nations as part of our inheritance and destiny. He longs to reveal His glory over the earth, as abundantly as the waters cover the sea. But He cannot do this if there is little fear of the Lord among His people. I believe before God reveals Himself and gives us the desires of His heart, a foundation must be laid. That foundation is the fear of the Lord. We cannot reach our destiny as individuals and as the Body of Christ without a fuller understanding and acceptance of God's greatness.

How can you tell if you are walking in the fear of God? One way is to look at your feelings when you think of your life and destiny. Are you in excited anticipation, or sunk in a state of ominous foreboding?

Here is one possible scenario:

"An exhilarating and personally fulfilling destiny awaits me. The same Creator who made the heavens and earth has also delicately fashioned me with a specific purpose in mind. He is constantly at work within me and around me, and I can sense His hand directing the unfolding stages of my life. His hopes and dreams, indeed the very expression of His heart, flows through me as I reveal His fragrant sweetness to a dying world."

Here is another possible scenario:

"I am struggling to keep my head above the water of difficult circumstances and have an ever-diminishing hope of finding my destiny. I believe there is a God, but He is not concerned with me. There is no connection between my everyday heartache and the God of the universe. I am resentful that I must follow obligatory Sunday rules and pay homage to the Christian religion. I understand that there are rules to follow, and I do the best I can by being a good person. When I die, I hope I go to heaven."

Which scenario best describes your thoughts about the life and destiny that awaits you? Personally, while growing up, much of my world was depicted in the second scenario. Inside of me I had a sense of a future, but I had no idea where to find it nor when I lost it. I couldn't see life apart from the rules and religion bordering my life. Now I realize that I had no direction because I did not possess a correct understanding of God. I would soon discover that my destiny was inextricably linked to the fear of the Lord. If you find hints of your thought pattern in the second scenario, then read on to discover the fear of God and prepare to reach your destiny.

Chapter Two

Moral Leadership

I can remember sitting around the dinner table with my family, and I was fuming with frustration. Being a senior in high school, life was simply not making sense to me. I asked my parents, "What is love?" This question summed up everything I couldn't understand.

To this day I cannot remember how my parents responded. I probably wouldn't have accepted their wisdom anyway. At that moment, I was struggling with the perennial questions of life, love, and relationships, and I couldn't put the pieces together in an orderly fashion or explain it to make sense. Is love the place to start? Is that all there is?

Greatest Commandment of All

As I grew older, I discovered I wasn't alone in my spiraling confusion. One of the scribes in the Bible questioned Jesus, "What command-ment is the foremost of all?"[13] This man was on a quest to understand the essential ingredi-ent for a relationship with God.

"Jesus answered, 'The foremost is, `Hear, O Israel! The Lord our God is one Lord; and you shall love the Lord your God with all your heart, and with all your soul, and with all your mind, and with all your strength. The second is this, `You shall love your neighbor as yourself.' There is no other commandment greater than these."[14]

For a greater part of my life, I thought Jesus meant that the emotion and action of love was the most important commandment to obey. Almost as easily as it rolls off the tongue, we don't think twice when we instruct our children that the greatest commandment is to love God, love your neighbors, and love yourself. Indeed, God himself is Love and He created humans in order to extend love to us. But are relationships only about love? Is love the only sermon Jesus was preaching? Let's look at how the scribe replied to Jesus:

"And the scribe said to Him, `Right, Teacher, You have truly stated that He is one; and there is no one else besides Him; and to love Him with all the heart and with all the understanding and with all the strength, and to love one's neighbor as himself is much more than burnt offerings and sacrifices.' And when Jesus saw that he had answered intelligently, He said to him, 'You are not far from the kingdom of God.' And after that, no one would venture to ask Him any more questions."[15]

Note that Jesus congratulated the scribe when he answered that the greatest commandment is: "He is one and there is no one else besides Him." Not, as I had previously thought, to love. Could it be that there is a divine order within relationships, especially when it pertains to our relationship with God? In the scripture above, Jesus clearly states we are to first acknowledge that He is God, and then love Him and other people.

A Divine Formula for Relationships

Let me draw an example. Let's say someone wants to have an intimate relationship with you. A very special someone; and this relationship will be based on mutual love and respect.

What would you say? What question would you ask?

Your immediate response would probably be, "Well, who is it?" We all understand that love within a relationship is a tangible expression of two people, and the nature of the parties involved will determine the type of love manifested. By knowing who this person is, you will know what type of love relationship will ensue.

• **If the person is a one-year old child.**
Since the physical nature of this child is very

young, he will have mental and physical limitations that clearly define the dynamics of the relationship. Within this relationship, you will play the role of the caretaker: changing diapers, feeding meals, and, probably, burping him afterwards.

• **If the person is a 16-year old teenager.**
This creates more exciting dynamics for the relationship (as compared to the previous example), and you will have increased expectations of your love being reciprocated. The teenager is beginning to define himself and has a greater capacity for choice, but he will still require guidance in certain areas.

• **If the person is a 49-year old parent.**
How you relate to this parent depends on how old you are. This person will have experienced some significant events to lend him authority in life. He will have formulated his own opinions and habits in certain areas of life. Being in a relationship with this person will require a heightened sense of maturity and responsibility, and in return, this relationship will also yield the highest degree of reciprocity.

Only when we have defined the nature of the "who" in the relationship, can we determine the dynamics of the association.

As it is with people, so it is with our relationship towards God. You must first know of

His greatness, position, or `nature' before you can properly relate to Him in the context of a relationship.

In other words, having a personal and accurate understanding of God's greatness is vital for us to define our relationship with Him. How does God portray Himself? How does He want to be related to? In the New Testament, the word "Lord" is used over 700 times, and the word "Savior" is used approximately 25 times. This should signal the priority in which God wants to be revealed; He is to be respected as Lord before He is appreciated for being our Savior. This is a matter of logic: it is difficult to respond appropriately to your Savior, if you don't understand that He is Lord. It is important to bear in mind that both attributes are important to understanding the fullness of God's character, but there does exist a divine order (or sequence) in which fallen man enters into an intimate relationship with God.

Moses: Understanding God's Nature and Character

Moses understood the primary importance of revering our awesome God.

As the Israelites were in the desert on their way to the Promised Land, they came upon an obstruction: the Red Sea. Moses prayed to God for help, and He answered by swiftly sweeping

the waters to either side, making a corridor of
dry ocean floor for the Israelites to pass safely
through. When the Israelites were feeling
parched and famished, Moses once again asked
the Lord for help, and He miraculously provided water from a rock and rained manna from
the sky. But the Israelites' faith in God was
short-lived. When Moses came down from
Mount Sinai, after being summoned to meet
with God for forty days, to his shock, in his
absence, the Israelites had fashioned a golden
calf and begun to worship it as an idol. In his
wrath, Moses pulverized the calf and threw it
in the stream. He then forced the Israelites to
drink the water to show them how powerless
thier god was.

Moses immediately returns up the mountain to
face God, and he writes:

"So I fell down before the Lord the forty days
and nights, which I did because the Lord had
said He would destroy you. And I prayed
to the Lord, and said, 'O Lord God, do not
destroy Thy people, even Thine inheritance,
whom Thou hast redeemed through Thy greatness, whom Thou has brought out of Egypt
with a mighty hand. Remember Thy servants,
Abraham, Isaac, and Jacob; do not look at the
stubbornness of this people or at their wick-
edness or their sin. Otherwise the land from
which Thou didst bring us may say, 'Because

the Lord was not able to bring them into the land which He had promised them and be-cause He hated them, He has brought them out to slay them in the wilderness.'"[16]

Moses' prayer reveals that his primary concern is for God's glory. If the Israelites could not be a testimony of the greatness of the Lord to the nations surrounding them, then Moses was afraid that God would be disgraced and disre-garded. In the above scripture, I have under-lined two of Moses' pleas towards God—notice that both petitions are concerned with hiding God's glory:

> 1. God was unable to bring them into the land;
> 2. God hated them.

The first reference indicates God's nature—the greatness, wisdom, and power that is inher-ent in the omnipotent One. If God was unable to bring the Israelites into the Promised Land, then He would not be God. God has infinite capacity, and to believe otherwise would be heresy. This revelation indicates that all honor and respect is due to God. Like Moses, we should be convinced that "God is one and there is no other God." Or, as the Lord re-vealed Himself at the burning bush, He is the great "I AM." To be concise, we must stand in awe of His greatness. The second reference speaks of God's character—the goodness and love that is inherent in Him. If God is Love, then He could not hate the Israelites.

God's greatness and goodness form the basis of God's glory. They are constantly and consistently repeated throughout the Bible.

This is what Jesus was talking about to the Scribe. He was saying to him, first recognize that God is great (One God) and then Love Him.

The chapter on faith, Hebrews 11, says, "And without faith it is impossible to please Him, for he who comes to God must believe that He is, and that He is a rewarder of those who seek Him."[17] Our faith must be rooted in the two pillars of God's greatness and goodness. Believing that "He is," presupposes that God is powerful and all encompassing, believing that "He is a rewarder," points to our belief that He will bestow goodness and justice.

Again we see the two pillars of faith appear in the book of Acts, as the church rapidly expands and continues toward her destiny. The church's formation and growth was rooted in her faith, as she actively walked and claimed God's greatness while being comforted by His love:

"So the church throughout all Judea and Galilee and Samaria enjoyed peace, being built up; and, going on in the fear of the Lord and in the comfort of the Holy Spirit, it continued to increase."[18]

The Psalmist beautifully portrays the dual tenets of God:

"But as for me, by Thine abundant lovingkindness I will enter Thy house. At Thy holy temple I will bow in reverence for Thee."[19]

"Once God has spoken; Twice have I heard this: That power belongs to God; And lovingkindness is Thine, O Lord, For Thou dost recompense a man according to his work."[20]

In Romans 1, the apostle Paul disputes the claim that ignorance of God excuses man from not fearing the Lord. He proposes that all of creation is a material expression of God's greatness, and since we bear witness to the tangible world, we are inherently obligated to revere God. He writes,

"For since the creation of the world His invisible attributes, His eternal power and divine nature, have been clearly seen, being understood through what has been made, so that they are without excuse. For even though they knew God, they did not honor Him as God, or give thanks; but they became futile in their speculations, and their foolish heart was darkened. Professing to be wise, they became fools."[21]

Paul highlights two foundational sins that demean God's nature and character. By not honoring God, we are irreverent towards His greatness, and by withholding gratitude, we ignore God's goodness. Again, God's greatness and goodness are the truths that form the basis of our faith; they are two legs on which we walk, led forth by our faith in Jesus Christ.

We can see these two truths utilized during election campaigns of politicians. Candidates will attempt to solicit votes by a platform based on their credentials of power (greatness) and goodness. Their agenda will first propose and promote the best course of legislation for a given issue, and second, convince the voters that they possess the capability to implement and enforce action.

Or, as another example, imagine yourself in a car wreck. You are alone and severely wounded, stranded on a deserted country road, and you must receive assistance immediately. You remember that back down the road is a friend who would do anything for you, but has no medical training. You also know that up the road is a capable medical doctor, but because of a longstanding family feud, he would love to seek revenge by hurting you.

If this situation is an either/or decision, you have a dilemma on your hands. Either you choose someone who wants to help but doesn't have the medical expertise, or you plead with someone who possesses the medical know-how but he refuses to help, or might even hurt you. In order to be healed, you must have both options. In other words, we need to look to those who possess power and will use it for our benefit.

God's Nature and Character Equals Reverential Fear

These two revelations of God's greatness and goodness are in healthy tension with each other. A.W. Tozer said, "Truth has two wings." It is imperative that we understand and respond appropriately to these foundational truths and once we do, God will release us into the fullness of His destiny for us.

Those who are rebellious and are actively involved in sin live in denial towards one or both of these truths. The following scriptures will give us a few examples:

"Woe to those who deeply hide their plans from the Lord, And whose deeds are done in a dark place, and they say, 'Who sees us?' or `Who knows us?'"[22]

"Then He said to me, 'The iniquity of the house of Israel and Judah is very great, and the land is filled with blood, and the city is full of perversion; for they say, `The Lord has forsaken the land, and the Lord does not see!'"[23]

"For the wicked boasts of his heart's desire, And the greedy man curses and spurns the

Lord. The wicked, in the haughtiness of his countenance, does not seek Him. All his thoughts are, 'There is no God.' Why has the wicked spurned God? He has said to himself, 'Though wilt not require it.'"[24]

Furthermore, when either one of these revelations are separated from the other, like a one-winged bird or a one-legged man, the Christian will find his capacity for a relationship with God limited.

• **If only the fear of God is emphasized**, without understanding God's love and goodness, then your perception of God will be distorted and you will think He is a demanding, unfeeling, wrathful God who must be obeyed. This relationship will cause you misery because you must work for His approval. God becomes a monster like Frankenstein in which fear is the all consuming essence of the relationship.

• **If only the love of God is emphasized,** devoid of reverence for an Almighty God, then your relationship with Him will end up in apathy and selfishness. He becomes a genie in a bottle, ready to answer your every whim and desire. Or you might portray him as a 365-day Santa Claus who will shower you with prosperity and blessings. This relationship will cause you to believe He is nothing but your best friend; and like a human being, will display areas of fallibility and impotence. This belief is sacrilegious and untrue and leads to bitter disappointment that God has not lived up to his supposed end of the bargain.

God desires a healthy combination of reverent intimacy. The clearer we understand His nature (i.e. greatness, power, and wisdom) the better we know how to respond to Him. You cannot have intimacy without knowing 'who' you are relating to. As we understand His greatness, we then discover how to relate to Him and can begin a journey of intimacy with Him. Our of the reverent intimacy we discover our destiny in God.

In summary, God is Big enough for any situation you face and Good enough to bring life out of any of our struggles.

Chapter Three

What is God's Nature Like?

We will never fully know.

Mighty Creator/ Awesome God

God is the Uncreated Creator and "his greatness is unsearchable."[25] His magnitude stretches clear beyond the boundaries of our imagination, and Infinitum can not be comprehended with finite minds. He says He is the Alpha and the Omega—the beginning and end—and since we are but a mere scratch on the infinite line of time, our vantage point is limited. It is only reasonable to assume that within the cavernous immensity of God are secrets we will never behold because they "belong to the Lord our God..."[26]

When I ponder upon the unknown, I find myself at once excited and terrified. There are even those who feel that God's infinite greatness only serves to create a sore point of frustration because it is too lofty for comprehension, beyond logic, and not computable. Thomas Carlyle speculates that "man's unhappiness…comes of his greatness; it is because there is an Infinite in him, which with all his cunning he cannot quite bury under the Finite."[27] In other words, our unhappiness is caused by our silly aspirations to define the infinite from within our finiteness. The solution is astoundingly simply: we must accept that this feat is impossible. If we will at once resolve to humility we would be more carefree, peaceful individuals. Our realization that "right is right, since God is God, and right the day must win; to doubt would be disloyalty, and to falter would be sin,"[28] unburdens our minds from having to figure things out. We contain evidence of the infinite within because we were made in the image of God; this unction should direct us towards God's greatness, and not towards ourselves.

This is how the apostle Paul concluded the mystery of God: "Oh the depth of the riches both of the wisdom and knowledge of God!" he exclaims, "how unsearchable are His judgments and unfathomable are His ways."[29] But, surely, it is the very nature of the enigma that perplexes, frustrates, and attracts our inquisitive minds towards God. King Solomon states that God (might) deliberately conceal a matter in order to solicit our attention and musings: "It is the glory of God to conceal a matter, but the glory of kings to search out a matter."[30] As a beautiful but mysterious girl will capture a man's heart, or as an intricate labyrinth of taxonomy might capture the anthropologist's attention, so to a significantly greater degree, the awesome and endless beauty of our God will capture our reverence forever.

To be released from the weight of understanding the enormity of God's nature is a considerable relief. And to be able to rejoice in His power and His greatness is a considerable joy. If His nature is as expansive as the Bible says—omnipotent, omniscient, and omnipresent—then I should have nothing to fear for my life! If I could anchor an unwavering faith in the solid knowledge that God is always present, always knowing, and the most powerful being of all, then the context of my life would be settled, and I can truly rest in peace. Here is another thought. If God was truly God, then we are not *supposed* to fully comprehend Him. Even Nietzsche, the staunch existentialist who declared that "God is dead," wrote: "whoever no longer finds greatness in God no longer finds it anywhere – he must either deny it or create it." Our yearning for infinity is not misplaced because our God is, indeed, infinite. But if we cannot be satisfied in God, then we will sacrilegiously create our own god to worship. This is idolatry, and an abomination to the Lord.

What else does the Bible tell us about God's greatness?

"Thus says the Lord, the King of Israel And his Redeemer, the Lord of hosts: 'I am the first and I am the last, And there is no God besides Me.'"[31]

"Before the mountains were born, Or Thou didst give birth to the earth and the world, Even from everlasting to everlasting, Thou art God."[32]

"It is He who sits above the vault of the earth, And its inhabitants are like grasshoppers, Who stretches out the heavens like a curtain, And spreads them out like a tent to dwell in."[33]

"'To whom then will you liken Me That I should be his equal?' says the Holy One. Lift up your eyes on high, And see who has created these stars, The One who leads forth their host by number, He calls them all by name; Because of the greatness of His might and the strength of His power, Not one of them is missing."[34]

The Heavens Declare His Glory

Emerson once said, "the stars awaken a certain reverence, because though always present, they are inaccessible."[35] Inaccessible, incredible, and from our point on earth, the stars are overwhelming indeed! God's nature is beyond our comprehension and we must suffice with only scratching the surface of His vastness. The Bible says that God "measured the waters in the hollow of His hand, and marked off the heavens by the span [of His hand]."[36] What is a span? The span is the distance between your thumb and baby finger, and if you stretch your fingers away from each other, this is how God measures the heavens. At best, what can we do with a span of our hand? Besides making an octave on the piano, our efforts are limited.

If we choose to believe in God's Word, then we must also believe that He holds (at least) all galaxies, all stars, and all planets in its personal and perfect place. Nor does God perform these luminous acts with herculean effort. In the same way we place our bag on the table and arrange our notepad and pens, is the same nonchalant ease with which He displays the dazzling objects of heaven. Awesome!

Living in Hawaii has spoilt me. I am treated to beautiful, balmy weather almost daily. Often I look up into the sky and marvel at the original artwork that is manifest. Sometimes the heavens will be an unblemished canvass of soft baby blue, at other times it will be streaked with interwoven laces of cirrus clouds, and just yesterday, it was occupied with billowing, angry fumes of grayish cumulus clouds. The skies alone are a testament to an artistic Creator who delights in unique designs, and will create them every day for the rest of eternity. But this is only the observation I receive in my backyard; what does the astronomer have to report about the heavens from the depths of his scientific laboratory?

'Speed of light,' as we learn, is the system of measurement we use for indicating distance in the universe. Light travels at 186,282.397 miles/ second. Light also travels approximately 5.9 trillion miles/ year. Using this system of measurement let's explore the depths of the heavens:

- **From the Earth, light will travel to the following heavenly bodies in approximately:**
    - 1.25 seconds to the Moon
    - 8 min. and 10.6 seconds to the Sun
    - 6 hours to Pluto
    - 4.28 light years to the nearest star
    - 75,000 light years to the most distant star in our Milky Way galaxy
    - 160,000 light years to the nearest extra galactic body (the larger Magellanic cloud)
    - 2,220,000 light years to Andromeda (the limit of naked eye vision)
    - 15,500,000 light years to edge of known universe in one direction.

- **The vastness of the universe as demonstrated by a paper stack model**
If the thickness of a sheet of paper = distance of Earth to Sun then:
    - to the nearest star = 71 foot high stack of paper

- to cover the diameter of Milky Way galaxy = 310 miles high stack of paper
- to reach the edge of the known universe = 31 million miles high stack of paper

• There are billions of times more stars in our universe than there are grains of sand on our Earth.

The better we understand the wonder of God's nature, the better we can appropriately respond to Him. As the revelation of His greatness graces our minds, I can guarantee you that our reverence for God will increase.

Imagine the scenarios below:

- treating a fire-cracker with the same reverence as a nuclear bomb.
- treating a model train with the same angst as a real oncoming train barreling down the train tracks
- treating a child's toy plane with the same wonder as a Boeing 747
- treating a bath tub's waves with the same respect as the 30 foot waves at high tide
- treating your next door neighbor with the same deference as the Prime Minister

In the above example, it would be ludicrous to treat each set of comparisons in the same way. Within each contrast there is a difference in magnitude, and each option is accorded the respect that is due to it. Neither is your show of respect one of sheer 'choice.' Granted, you could ignore the oncoming train or the 30-foot tsunami surf, but you would be toast if you do so. Although you are technically free to choose your response, theoretically there is only one wise choice, and in the case of the speeding train and crashing wave it would be to get away, fast. As it is in the material world, so it is in our relationship with God. The amount of respect we credit to God should be in proportion to the amount of respect He deserves. And God deserves all glory and honor and praise. We can willingly make the wise choice to accord Him greatness now. There would be no detriment in this decision, only benefits of infinite magnitude. But if you choose our own way, eventually, when God reveals His glory over the earth, every knee will be compelled to bow and every tongue will confess that Jesus Christ is Lord.

"Who would not fear Thee, O King of the nations? Indeed it is Thy due! For among all the wise men of the nations, And in all their kingdoms, There is none like Thee."[37]

Chapter Four

An Appropriate Response to God

In light of the magnificent context of God's
greatness, the wisest 'choice' is to respond to
God accordingly. Whether it is with solemn
dignity, silent admiration, or an overwhelming
ecstatic shout, gratitude and, inevitably, humility will naturally arise within us. "When I
consider Thy heavens, the works of Thy fingers, The moon and the stars, which Thou hast
ordained," proclaims the Psalmist, "What is
man, that Thou dost take thought of him? And
the son of man, that Thou dost care for him?"[38]
Like King David, it is incomprehensible to me
that God does take notice of us. In fact, this
verse—"What is man, that Thou dost take
thought of him?"—is in large lettering, carved
atop one of Harvard University's library, the
U.S. institution that has educated and hosted
some of time's most brilliant minds. These
scholars, replete with their wealth of knowledge, believe that the end of man's wisdom is
the beginning of humility. He who measures
the heavens by the span of His hand is a truly
glorious and awesome God, and incomparable
in wisdom. If the heavens declare the glory

of God, what then would be our appropriate response? Does our understanding of God's greatness create an obligation for humanity? If so, what is it?

We will worship an object as much as we are convinced it has value. A.W. Tozer argues that unless we are convinced that God is who He says He is, and for the greatness that He embodies, we will always be shortchanging our lives and the reverence due Him. Tozer writes:

"What comes into our minds when we think about God is the most important thing about us. The history of mankind will probably show that no people has ever risen above its religion, and man's spiritual history will positively demonstrate that no religion has ever been greater than its idea of God. Worship is pure or based on the worshipper entertaining high or low thoughts of God.

For this reason the gravest questions before the church is always God Himself, and the most portentous fact about any man is not what he at a given time may say or do, but what he in his deep heart conceives God to be like. We tend by secret law of the soul to move towards our mental image of God...Were we able to extract from any man a complete answer to the question, 'What comes into your mind when you think of God?' we might predict with certainty the spiritual future of that man."[39]

As our understanding of God becomes clearer, there is a growing obligation felt in the heart of man. What is that obligation? Charles Finney, the great revivalist, made a statement: "intrinsic value obligates." In simple terms, Finney is saying that we have the obligation, or the responsibility, to respond to the perceived value of something. Let's discuss this in greater length by means of a practical example.

Perception vs. Reality

Imagine that I have in my right hand a dime and in my left hand a one-dollar bill. If there are no other values attached to the coins (e.g. the dime is a rare dime), which would you choose?

But, of course, you would choose the one-dollar bill. You would choose this every time, and so would I, and every one else. In this case, the process of making a choice between two objects is the process of discerning these objects' value. Discerning value and the choice of the higher value cannot be separated from each other. When we find an object of greater value over something of lesser value, it is immediately clear which choice to make. Now if I added a ten-dollar bill in my left hand with the one-dollar bill, would this additional amount change your choice? If I added a hundred-dollar bill in my left hand and the dime is still in my other hand, would you change your choice? No, in fact the greater the value differences the easier the choice. Thus, the greater the value of one object over the other, the greater the 'obligation' I have to choose it. You are not overwhelmed by such a choice. It does not cause you stress or indecision because it is an easy choice. Thus when an object's values are clearly established a decision can be easily made.

The primary reason it is difficult to make choices is because our knowledge is finite and we assess objects by our "perceived" value. Our perception is a personal assessment. It is our attempt to make the right choice as seen through our experiences, memories, personality, and culture. But even at the very best, our knowledge is limited and our assessments are biased.

In order to explain "perceived value," let's extend the above illustration. What would happen if I changed the currency of the money? Now, I have one thousand Indonesian Rupiahs in my left hand and one U.S. dollar in my right hand—which hand would you choose? The choice is still possible, if given enough time to learn the exchange rate of Rupiahs to U.S. Dollar, but the immediacy and the clear choice has disappeared. The choice becomes harder to make. We now have additional values attached to the objects to further complicate the choice. These may be some possible considerations: you can spend the dollar easier; you are more interested in the novelty of owning Indonesian Rupiahs; you are living in Indonesia so Rupiahs are more practical; or what if the particular Rupiah note is a collector's item?

Therefore, if we are not comparing apples to apples and artichokes to artichokes, how do we determine an object's value? And how do we find an object's value without the limitations of our finite perceptions?

Determination of Value

(Interjection: I fear I will make this sound like an Economics 101 class if I stray too far from our idea of the fear of the Lord. But if you will indulge me, and understand the following analogy, I promise there is a clear payoff.)

When you go shopping to buy a product, how do you determine what you are willing to pay? Remember the words "worth," "cost," and "value" are synonyms for this discussion. There are, at least, four aspects that will aid you in (consciously or sub-consciously) determining an object's value, and what you will pay for it.

1) Quantity/ Unique:
In the proverbial "supply and demand" graph, this would be the "supply" aspect. If the object you wanted to purchase was a 'limited supply'

item, how would the dearth of the object reflect in its value? Commonly, if something is rare or hard to find, then its value will be higher. Inversely, if this product is produced in massive quantities, if it is available on every shelf in many stores, then you can assume it would be cheaper than if it were less in quantity.

2) Beauty/ Aesthetically Appealing:
Although beauty is often in the eye of the beholder and different expressions of beauty appeal to different people, there is an inherent element of beauty and attractiveness that we recognize and appreciate. Usually, the more beautiful something is, and the better its powers to arrest our steps and capture our gaze, the higher its value will be. This is why we will deliberately stop what we are doing in order to watch a beautiful sunset (especially the spectacular ones in Kailua-Kona where I live) and attempt to catch it on film to prolong the memory. Beautiful sunsets are valuable, even a two-dimensional representation of the real thing—this is the premise of postcard selling.

3) Quality/ Purity/ Long Lasting:
If you knew that an object was pure and the quality of it was such that it would never break or wear out, what would happen to its value? The purer or better quality an object is, the higher it's worth. This is why a 24-carat gold ring is more valuable than a 14- or 18-carat ring because the higher the carat, the purer the gold

content, and the less alloyed metals there are within the ring. Designer items are expensive because it has a "lifetime guarantee," these objects command a higher price because it will last a lifetime, and on the off chance it doesn't last, it will get replaced.

4) Need/ Want:
This fourth aspect is tricky because sometimes it is hard to distinguish between 'need' and 'want.' What would your choice be if I asked, "Would you rather have a million dollars or air to breathe?" Unless you could get a lifetime's worth of pleasure between thirty seconds and a minute, the need for air would force you to choose oxygen over money.

As aforementioned, all our choices are rooted in the perception of value, and our responsibility to choose the "best" value. Personal preferences are an ingredient within perceived values, but there are also values that are common to a society e.g. the legislative law. The standard for defining humanity lies in our choices. This is a key part of what it means to be made in the image of God. God made choices based on value and calls us to do the same.

God's Choice

Obviously, unlike us, God is not limited by finite perception. God does not struggle to find out the truth because He knows everything. In this case, what has God found to be of great value? And is God 'free' from the obligation of choosing what is most valuable?

Let's look at the book of Job to discover the answer. In chapter 28, Job investigates men's capabilities. He determines that men can put an end to darkness, overturn mountains, dam up streams, and find precious metals. We know where to search for sapphires, gold and other treasures that no other animal can find. In fact, there even exists a great temptation to think we can discover what is of great value by ourselves.

But Job asks one questions that speaks of the heart of our struggle. In verses 12 and 13, he realizes that we can find most valuable things, but not *the* most valuable thing: wisdom. "But where can wisdom be found? And where is the place of understanding? Man does not know its value, Nor is it found in the land of the living." We can find things of perceived value around us, but we don't know the real value of it from Wisdom's perspective. Only wisdom can provide the bigger picture. Job determines that all the precious jewels around us is not enough to pay for the wisdom we need. We cannot find the wisdom we need in the land of the living, says Job. There is a note of despair, but he is not cast down. For Job adds at the end:

"God understands its way; And He knows its place. For He looks to the ends of the earth, And sees everything under the heavens. When He imparted weight to the wind, And meted out the waters by measure, When He set a limit for the rain, And a course for the thunderbolt, Then He saw it and declared it; He established it and also searched it out. And to man He said, 'Behold, the fear of the Lord, that is wisdom; And to depart from evil is understanding.'"[40]

In essence, God reassures us that He who created the heavens, has searched it out on our behalf, and can authoritatively tell us that nothing is more valuable than Him. God, and the fear of Him, is the beginning of wisdom.[41] God is the I AM for the past, the I AM for the current, and the I AM for the future; at every point in time, God is in the present, holding the universe together by His power. If God were to withdraw His sustaining power at any point, the universe would collapse.

Andrew Murray, in his book "Humility" puts it this way:

"The relationship of man to God could only be one of dependence. As truly as God by His power once created, so truly by that same power must God, every moment, maintain. Man need only look back to the origin of existence and he will acknowledge that he owes everything to God."[42]

God is the most humble being in the universe and in all humility He says to creation: "I AM it." This is not a statement of pride, but a statement of fact. He knows His nature is unique, beautiful, and essential for mankind. And in answer to our previous question, yes, God is also 'bound' to choosing what is most valuable in the universe—and so He chooses Himself.

Reverential Response to His Value

If these assumptions about God's value are applied to our example, our paradigm would look like this:

1) Unique:
God's nature is unique. We could search out the whole universe for all eternity and there would never, ever, be anyone or anything like Him.

"Thus says the Lord, the King of Israel And his Redeemer, the Lord of hosts: 'I am the first and I am the last, And there is no God besides Me.'"[43]

"Do not tremble and do not be afraid; Have I not long since announced it to you and declared it? And you are My witnesses. Is there any God besides Me, Or is there any other Rock? I know of none."[44]

"For thus says the Lord, who created the heavens (He is the God who formed the earth and made it, He established it and did not create it a waste place, But formed it to be inhabited), 'I am the Lord, and there is none else.'"[45]

2) Beauty:
A Creator cannot create something that is more beautiful than His imagination. If we could capture every sweet aroma, every iridescent color, every satin texture, and every melliflu-ous melody and concentrate it in a capsule, then if we amplified the intensity a billion-fold, we would only be touching the hem of His beauty.

3) Quality/ Purity:
God is pure, and He is eternal. If we took all the grains of sand in the world and let it drop through an hourglass at the rate of one grain/ million years, eternity would only begin after all the sand of the earth ceased dripping.

"In the beginning God created the heavens and the earth."[46]

"Before the mountains were born, Or Thou didst give birth to the earth and the world, Even from everlasting to everlasting, Thou art God."[47]

4) Need/ Want:
If God were to withdraw His power from the universe it would immediately return to dust.

His power holds the universe together, and all creation looks to Him as the source of life. As the old hymnals read, "I need Thee every hour" and it is God who "lendest us our every breath."

"For by Him all things were created, both in the heavens and on earth, visible and invisible, whether thrones or dominions or rulers or authorities—all things have been created by Him and for Him. And He is before all things, and in Him all things hold together."[48]

Against the backdrop of the mighty universe, with the very galaxies, stars, and planets dangling as mere props, the actors and actresses must now choose the script. God, after all, gave us a free will. Do we choose His script? Do we even want a part in God's play? Like the woman who has been charmed by her lover, she must respond to his question: "Will you have me?" This is a personal question for each of us. Dear reader, I ask you: will you have God?

If you have followed my arguments for determining God's value, you will realize that you need Him, but maybe you can't work up the feeling to *want* God. At this point, you must pray what Tozer prayed: God, give me a desire to desire you more. I encourage you to ask God for a revelation of how much you want Him in your life.

"The kingdom of heaven is like a treasure hidden in the field, which a man found and hid; and from joy over it he goes and sells all that he has, and buys that field. Again, the kingdom of heaven is like a merchant seeking fine pearls, and upon finding one pearl of great value, he went and sold all that he had, and bought it."[49]

The part that particularly fascinates me about this parable is the man's excessive "joy" that makes him sell all his possessions. This is not the Christianity we are commonly taught. For "joy?" What joy? We don't sell our livelihood, because we think that our livelihood is all we have to hold on to, and it is more valuable to us than any other thing. This is the painful, distorted part of contemporary Christianity. Whole congregations will bypass God and go straight to religion, its dogma, customs, and image. We try to be good, inevitably fail, and quickly become a victim to our small and ever diminishing value. In a desperate haste to increase our value, we rely on our actions and works to justify our lives, and here hails the quick demise of life, love, and laughter, the very crux of God's religion.

Our perceptions would massively change if we saw the value of God. In simple pictorial form, here is the value of God, and the value of man. (He is much bigger than this, but I am limited by the size of the paper).

Value of God   Value of a man

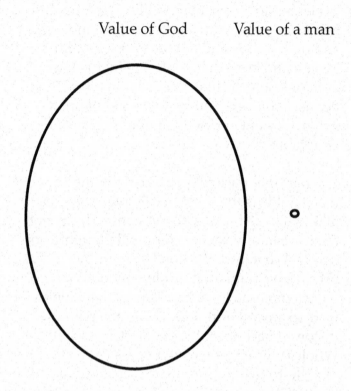

This is a simple test: which is bigger? Which should you be more interested in? Because intrinsic value—the bigger circle—obligates, you are responsible for choosing the object of greater value. Here is what Paul wrote in his testimony about his own value in light of Jesus' value:

"But whatever things were gain to me, those things I have counted as loss for the sake of Christ. More than that, I count all things to be loss in view of the surpassing value of know-

ing Christ Jesus my Lord, for whom I have suffered the loss of all things, and count them but
rubbish in order that I may gain Christ."[50]

The original Greek word that Paul used for
"rubbish" actually means refuse, animal excrement, and dregs. Here was a man who could
have boasted about his leadership, self-righteousness and zeal before all people. But to
him, there is no comparison between God's
value system and his own (which he calls
'dung'). Like Paul, we should realize that
Christ's value outweighs anything and everything.

The Psalmist also wrote of our responsibility to
choose God's value:

"Ascribe to the Lord, O sons of the mighty,
Ascribe to the Lord glory and strength. Ascribe
to the Lord the glory due to His name."[51]

To have great reverence for something is to see
its value. If you don't see God's nature and
His value you will have little reverence for
Him. And if we miss the revelation of God's
value, then we will choose something of lessor
value, which is foolishness.

"O sons of men, how long will my honor become a reproach? How long will you love what
is worthless and aim at deception?"[52]

"Thus they exchanged their glory for the image of an ox that eats grass."[53]

"Has a nation changed gods, When they were not gods? But My people have changed their glory for that which does not profit."[54]

"Thus says the Lord, 'What injustice did your fathers find in Me, That they went far from Me and walked after emptiness and became empty?'"[55]

"For many walk, of whom I often told you, and now tell you even weeping, that they are enemies of the cross of Christ, whose end is destruction, whose god is their appetite, and whose glory is in their shame, who set their minds on earthly things."[56]

These desolate scriptures can be compared with the hopeful, ecstatic verses that we find in Revelations. They joyously ring forth: Worthy is the Lamb to receive all blessing, honor, glory and power..."[57]

The Psalmist had a clear understanding of God's greatness when he made this commitment—"I will set no worthless thing before my eyes; I hate the work of those who fall away; It shall not fasten its grip on me."[58]

A fuzzy understanding of God's nature and greatness will blur our picture of God. We remind ourselves of Tozer's insight: "We tend by secret law of the soul to move towards our mental image of God." If in our deepest heart we should only consider, if in our mind's eye we should only see, if in our sense we feel that God should be attributed the highest honor, then we will *automatically* manifest reverent actions according to His greatness. A key part of our work is to give God what is due Him. Nothing more, and nothing less. Although we will soon realize that we can never give God more than what He deserves; He deserves our very lives.

Imagine someone you know who has an item of great value to them. How does he treat his esteemed object...

- With cautious concern? Maybe over bearing attention? (He doesn't want to lose it)
- With a heartfelt devotion? Some ex pression of 'worship' towards it? (He adores it)
- Protecting it? Guarding it from harm and dirt and potential negative influences? (He wants it in safe keeping)
- Displaying it with pride? Wanting to be connected with it? (He believes it's worthy of praise)

- Genuinely shocked, or offended when others don't appreciate its worth? (He wonders how others cannot see its value)

Now question yourself: does the world see these characteristics in us as we relate to God? If they don't, then there is little fear of God within us and around us, and we must call out to God to grace us with a greater revelation of Himself. As we learned from Chapter One, if there is no fear of God, then we will lose our destiny.

Oh God,
We are a people that are easily distracted and quickly impressed with things that are not eternal. We want just enough of you to make us feel warm and comforted, but not so much that will make us squirm or do things that might embarrass us before our friends and family. We are not yet the enamored lover who will go to great lengths for his love. This only reveals that we are playing religion and have little knowledge of who you really are. Would you break forth into our world, and create opportunities so that we can know more of you? Reveal yourself so that we are forever undone and in awe of you! Save us from ourselves, and our distractions and limitations, so that we might know you as you truly are. This is my prayer and desire. In Jesus' name. Amen.

Chapter Five

Battle for Context

A few years ago, my wife Celia sold jewelry as a part time job and did exceedingly well. So well, in fact, that the company helped her purchase a new car. The only requirement was that the car had to be a luxury model. Without further ado, Celia, who has exquisite taste, picked out a sleek silver Jaguar. It was beautiful, and not a little unbelievable for us because we had live without a fixed income in a missions agency our whole married life. Our other car was a humble 1989 Toyota Tercel. The roof of the car toted a surf rack from the previous owner. Salt water would drip off the boards, and create blotchy rust spots on the car. The tired engine was slowly losing power, and gradually, it even blew smoke out of its tail as it puttered down the road. After this conveyance, owning the Jaguar was a treat.

As I brandished our new car, and carefully and slowly meandered it through the streets of downtown Kailua-Kona, I was amazed at the attention that I solicited. Pedestrians would blatantly peer through my windshields to catch a glimpse of me, the driver of the beautiful car. Other cars would defer to me, and even – I was convinced – the sun shone brighter upon the polished paint of my Jaguar. "Hey!" I thought, "I am somebody when I drive this car." The next day I drove my Toyota, and I got a nasty shock. The fickle pedestrians that had only a a day before turned their face towards my car are now uncaring, the cars that had previously deferred to me were ready to run me over, and it seemed to rain on the day I drove my Toyota. I felt like a nobody. It was then that I clearly realized I was projecting my self-value on the car I was driving. When I was encased in the leather seats of the Jaguar, I was king of the jungle; when I was wedged in the seat of the Toyota, I was a lowly prey, vulnerable and afraid.

Now a strange thing happened when I drove our Jaguar around our missions campus. My feelings were reversed. In a place where there are mostly volunteers, there is a subtle, yet very real, value placed on being "poor" and living by 'faith.' When I drove my Toyota on campus, my modest car was at home and ac-cepted by the community. When I drove my Jaguar onto the campus, I saw stifled horrified looks and I felt embarrassed and out of place. I must admit I was glad when we exchanged the Jaguar for another car; I wasn't able to handle the mixed value system.

Upon retrospection, I realized that the tension of owning such a high profile 'status' symbol was symptomatic of a bigger problem. It revealed the warring values within myself. This struggle of tension is common to all man. It is the heart of the struggle upon which our very survival depends. There is no neutral ground, and there are no 'safe' zones that are free from the conflict of values. This is why the Bible tells us to watch over our heart with all diligence for from it flows the springs of life. It also tells us that where your "treasures" are, there will your heart be also.

The world pushes certain values on the individual. For some of us, One set of designer clothes makes us 'feel' valuable, and for others being seen in a certain restaurant makes us feel good. We want to drive a certain car or have a certain position in an organization. A week hardly goes by when we are not challenged to find our value in what we have, where we are, who we are friends with, or what we look like. If we will be truthful with ourselves, our deceitful heart will place value in things around us and to the degree we buy the lie, to that degree it will be our downfall. The Jaguar brought me value, but the Jaguar also brought me headaches beyond measure because I had to battle with the morality of my appearances. I have a friend who recently graduated from Princeton, a prestigious Ivy League university in the US. She claimed that she found her value in Princeton, and to that degree, it also brought her grief beyond measure because she had to continually validate herself through academic recognition.

So why not escape the despotism and the stupidity of the inflated or propped up values that are exerted upon us? Although they will always be among us, we have a choice to reject these social mores. We are in a battle of values. In military terms this battle is called "comprehensive situational awareness" and "precision engagement." Billions of dollars are spent and hundreds of satellites deployed to give a clear context and remove what the 19th-century theorist Carl von Clausewitz called 'fog' and 'friction.'[59] If the enemy is lost in a fog of limited information and the friction of the conflict is not clear, his capacity to survive is limited. Getting a clear overhead view will remove the problem.

In our "modern" western view, relativism is the fog that is hiding the life of our nation and allowing room for the enemy to destroy us. It is the friction point that is killing us from within. Relativism is the view that there is no absolute 'truth,' 'value,' or context and that everything is 'relative.' Each person defines life as he sees it or wants to see it, and he is accountable to no other individual. If a pervasive relativistic attitude exists, then people will create their own values. Whatever they create is reality, and this reality is their 'truth.' Truth, then, only becomes your perception of reality. It does not take much extrapolation to conclude that relativism will lead to vastly diverging realities, and eventual chaos.

The same friend who attended Princeton also majored in English Literature. She told me of how the religion of relativism ruled in her class, and after three hours of discussion, she would feel uncommonly bewildered and annoyed at the wasted time and effort. When there is no basis of truth or when arguments do not stem from the same foundation, then the issue is null and void before it has even started. It is like arguing whether Shakespeare's works are better than Sylvia Plath's, or whether one can compare the pathetic fallacy found in Jane Austen and Dr. Seuss. It is idiotic futility because there is no basis for comparison. As long as people are arguing from their, separate, versions of "truth," it is reasonable to assume they will argue themselves into a cotton wool.

A person may get cancer and after the doctor reports the "bad news," he immediately operates to remove the malignant cells. We define the cancer as evil. Yet, to argue from the cancer's point of view, it is the doctor who is evil for killing the cancerous cells. Depending on the perspective, any issue can be argued one way or the other.

But this does not mean that every perspective is necessarily correct. Even if the majority argues for a wrong viewpoint, it does not make the viewpoint right. 'Right' and 'wrong' should not be based on limited views, personal preference, utilitarianism, or fancy rhetoric, because if it were, than the brutal actions of Hitler, Mussolini, and Pol Pot would have been `right.' There will always be multiple perspectives. But there can only be one context in which to judge whether the different perspectives are closer or farther from reality. It is vital to understand this particular context, so allow me to make myself as clear as possible.

The Importance of a Context

As I had mentioned, there are many different perspectives, but only one 'context.' The word "context" in the dictionary is defined as:

1. parts surrounding a word, sentence, or passage which help determine the meaning: *to quote*
2. *a passage out of context.* 2. Surroundings; environment [Latin *contextus* a joining together, connection, going back to *con* – together + *texere* to weave.][60]

If you are reading a novel and come across a word you don't understand, and you did not have a dictionary easily available, what would you do? You would probably try to understand the word by reading the context that it is in, that is, the sentence, paragraph and even the story in order to understand the word. The overall picture of where the word fits in is the context for its use and meaning. If you can't understand the word, you must fit it in a 'context' that helps define it. Words have a certain meaning depending on the context they are contained within. In speech, the tone, speed, facial contortions, and body movements all influence the meaning of the words.

For example, read the sentence below four times, each time with a different emphasis on a word, so the first time the emphasis would be on "I," and then "can't," and so on and so forth.

"I can't do that!"

As you can hear, by emphasizing different words within the same sentence, the implications are vastly different. Is this a statement of refusal? Is it a moral conviction? Is it a statement about limitations? Is it rebellion? Is it a statement about inferiority or a lack of self-image? Is it a statement about gifts and ministry? Is it a subtle way of inviting more conversation?

You can't know the meaning of the sentence until you hear a context in which it is spoken, or see it in which it is written. Researchers tell us that 72% to 86% of all communication is nonverbal. This indicates that most of a word's meaning and implications must be derived from the context. Here are three examples for which the above sentence, "I can't do that!", can be appropriated. You will notice that the connotations are different because of the context:

• This statement is a protest from an employee who has been requested by his boss to deliberately deceive his wife. This boss wants his subordinate to say that he's gone on a business trip, when he has really gone off on a romantic rendezvous with his new girlfriend. In this case, the sentence is exclaimed 'morally.'

• This statement is made by a sullen teenage daughter who has been told by her mother to go clean her room. In this case, the sentence has been said in rebellion.

• This statement is a response from someone who is cooking when asked to pick up the telephone. In this case, the sentence has been uttered as a matter of physical limitations.

The context gives understanding to the meaning of the words. When you get the context, you can then understand the emphasis and intention of the words. You can have different perspectives on the meaning of words, but when you know the context for the words you will then, and only then, be able to understand the intent.

As it is with words so it is with our lives. A context for our lives will give us an indication of what is valuable. In a world with millions of voices and perspectives and attractive possibilities, what do we use to tie together all of the different perspectives? Who defines what the context is?

Chapter Six

What Did We Lose In Our Rebellion?

When God first created Adam and Eve, He intended to have an intimate and loving relationship with them. This would be an association of mutual attraction, where He would extend Himself—Love—to the man and woman, and arising from free will, they would choose to love Him in return. But when Adam and Eve took their eyes off of God, and chose to actively rebel against His commands, they were banished from the physical presence of God. Their exile from the Garden of Eden was the immediate practical consequence of sin, but what serious implications did this separation have on the rest of their lives? And what is our modern day 'inheritance' in the Rebellion? We were born into a fallen world, but until we understand what we lost, we will not know what we are trying to find.

Let us begin by looking at God's communication with fallen man. His first interaction is, interestingly enough, not a statement, but a question. He asks Adam and Eve, "Where are you?" Assuming that God is omniscient, and therefore knew where they were hiding, why did He choose to ask a question? God is more interested in allowing us to understand where we are in relation to Him, rather than condemning our strayed position. Our rebellion gave birth to a distorted context for which our lives operate. In other words, like a car in thick midst, we don't know where we are, and we have lost the meaning and context for our lives. Humbly admitting to our 'lostness' is the foundation by which we can recapture, or 'find,' a context for understanding our lives.

Here is an example. Suppose your friend wants to visit you and rings you to ask for directions. In order to start directing him, you must begin with the question, "Where are you?" Based on where he is, you can give him directions to get to your house. These directions must be relevant within the context of where he is. It would be useless to give him directions from the east, if he lives to the west of you. As a result of Adam and Eve's rebellion, we have lost the clear context of our lives.

The New Testament describes our loss of context as 'darkness': "And this is the judgment, that the light is come into the world, and men loved the darkness rather than the light; for their deeds were evil."[61] For rebellious mankind, the enticement of darkness is when it enshrouds and obliterates the light. The comfort of darkness is that it removes the context. A misconception arises that we have the discretion and freedom to create any context we choose. A particular illustration by Norman Rockwell comes to my mind at this point. It is a picture of a cross section of society—old men, young children, middle aged housewives—and the heading reads: "Each to the Dictates of His Own Conscience." This statement is theoretically sound, and it is the very bedrock of our democratic institution. But there is also an inherent danger. If each man is dictated to act according to his own conscience, then there would be no uniformity of right and wrong, and lawlessness would be rampant. If context is what you choose, then the only benchmark for rightness is whatever feels 'good.' Currently we hail this as arbitrary relativism, in the future, we might decry it as social anarchy.

Shedding light is the same as surrounding an action, attitude or word within a context. All things become visible when they are exposed. When actions, attitudes, and words are illuminated, they are evaluated within the context. In our particular case, the context that we are interested in is the Biblical framework, or truth, as instructed by God. "But he who practices the truth comes to the light, that his deeds may be manifested as having been wrought in God."

To further explore the importance of context, let's take for example the action below:

I reach into the biscuit tin and take a biscuit.

It would be impossible to ask you for a value judgement on this action. As far as you know, this action takes place in a vacuum. I have not exposed the context of this action, and in a sense, it is done in 'darkness.' But look what happens when I begin to add context for texture:

I have just walked through the front door and am a little hungry, and I reach into the biscuit tin and take a biscuit.

How does it look now? Nothing wrong at all; it sounds normal. But maybe there is more information I have not divulged...

I am a burglar and I intend to break into someone's house to steal his possessions. I have just walked through the front door and am a little hungry, and I reach into the biscuit tin and take a biscuit.

Now what happens when you see the bigger picture of who I am and what I am doing? This information creates a 'context' in which you can appropriately evaluate the action. As it is with this action, so it is with each thought, attitude and life that is lived. Each is done in a context and can be evaluated based within the context.

God helps us set a context, and He does this by enabling us to understand where we are. Not just where we are geographically or emotionally, but where we are spiritually, and specifically, *in relation to Him.* Remember He is the most valuable being in the universe. Thus He is reality. It means understanding the context, taking responsibility for our choices within the context, and adjusting our choices to align with God's. This, my dear reader, is a monumental task. In each step we must show a greater degree of humility – in the act of admittance, in consequent repentance, and continued obedience to His will. Adam and Even knew they had sinned. But instead of admitting, repenting, and obeying, Eve blamed the snake, Adam blamed Eve, both indirectly blamed God, and they struggled to accept the context that confronted them. It was critical for them to accept God's context; it is just as critical now.

This struggle for defining a context can be found throughout the Bible:

- Cain declared, "Am I my brother's keeper?"[62] He didn't want to be responsible for the murder of his brother, Abel.
- Sarah laughed at the thought of her as an old woman giving birth, even though

God has specifically promised to give her a child. She refused to see things from God's perspective and His might.[63]

- Abram also showed disrespect towards God by not believing Sarah could conceive a child. He ventures out of God's context and conceives a child through his servant, Hagar.[64]
- Esau sold his birthright to Jacob.[65] He did not value the things that God placed value on.
- Jacob deceived his father for what should have been Esau's blessing.[66]
- Joseph's brothers sold him into slavery and told their father that Joseph was dead.[67] They didn't like the fact that their younger brother had power over them.
- Pharaoh refused to let the Israelites leave Egypt.[68] He thought his position gave him the power to reign supreme, even over God's commands.

The list continues. Each person attempted to redefine the context according to his or her own strength and capabilities, thereby hoping to disable God's sovereignty. There was no fear of the Lord in their hearts.

During Joshua's reign, the Gibeonites heard about Israel and their powerful God, and they were terrified.[69] They knew God would help Israel destroy Gibeon and conquer all the sur-

77

rounding kingdoms as well. So they decided to trick the Israelites into making peace with them. As a way of distorting the context, they put on bedraggled looking rags and carried with them what appeared to be old and moldy goods. These aged artifacts were 'witness' to the claim that they had come from a distant land.

The men of Israel suspected that these men were deceiving them, but the Gibeonites denied it. They 'proved' the distance they traveled by displaying old food and clothes. In Joshua 9:14-15 the text reads, "So the men of Israel took some of their provisions, and did not ask for the counsel of the Lord. And Joshua made peace with them and made a covenant with them, to let them live; and the leaders of the congregation swore an oath to them."

Joshua and the leaders assumed they could use their own judgements to determine the context of the situation, even though in actuality they had very limited information. By not consulting the Lord, they chose to remove the fear of God from their circumstance, and because they trusted in their own strength and knowledge, they lost part of the inheritance that God had planned to bless them with.

As has now been determined, not only is the 'context' important, but so is the authority figure who defines the framework. The Israelites should have consulted God's counsel because He possesses omniscient knowledge and is willing to give us wisdom if we ask for it. "But if any of you lacks wisdom, let him ask of God, who gives to all men generously and without reproach, and it will be given to him."[70]

So what happens when we disregard the fear of God, and do not allow His tenet to set our context?

The World as a Context

If we don't have the fear of the Lord as our context then the world will create a context out of which we will live. Either we act in God's power and determine to follow His principles, or else we will be acted upon by the world. In our human minds, we must have a context from which to live. And if it is not already filled with God's truths, then it creates a vacuum for which we allow the world to dictate our values and benchmarks of success. The Bible shows us that the 'world' has a system that is against God, and it is all, ultimately, dictated by Satan, who is the prince of this world.

"No one can serve two masters; for either he will hate the one and love the other, or he will hold to one and despise the other. You cannot serve God and mammon."[71]

"For all that is in the world, the lust of the flesh and the lust of the eyes and the boastful pride of life, is not from the Father, but is from the world."[72]

It is important to note that when we are encouraged to reject the world's system, we should not reject the world. God created the tangible, material world as an expression of His love, beauty, and creativity—and He deemed that His work was "good." Therefore we shouldn't disdain any profession as being 'unholy,' nor should we reject anyone as being impossible to bring to salvation. In fact, we should consider all things as only having been perverted from its original, good purpose. Our goal is to redeem areas of the world back for God. So we are not rejecting the world and its inhabitants, but its false value system.

Religion as a Context

Religion is another context by which people will feel tempted to base their lives in, for example, Islam or Buddhism. But if you are reading this book, these religions are probably not personally applicable. Your struggle will lean towards legalism and religiosity in Christianity. If you ever overlook God's nature and character, and forget that He is the Christ of whom Christianity is centered on, then you will use religious modes as a way of controlling your life. After being in the missions field for over two decades, and watching many Christians struggle to be 'good' and follow the rules and regulations of Christian doctrine, I can testify that if you try to define yourself by using religion it will eventually destroy you and those around you. W. Barclay delineates the challenge that the Scribes and Pharisees had to keep the Ten Commandments. Although he writes in a serious manner, you will notice that after awhile the rigid and endless rules become, poignantly, amusing.

"'REMEMBER THE SABBATH DAY TO KEEP IT HOLY.' Became in the Mishnah 24 chapters, (on one of which a certain famous rabbi spent two and a half years in detailed study). In the Jerusalem Talmud it became 64 and a half columns, and in the Babylonian Talmud it occupies a hundred and fifty-six double folio pages.

How then did the scribes proceed? The commandment says that there must be no work on the Sabbath. The scribe immediately asks: 'What is work?' Work is then defined under 39 different heads which are called 'fathers of work.' One of the things which is forbidden is the carrying of a burden. Immediately the scribe asks: 'What is a burden?' So in the Mishnah there is definition after definition of what constitutes a burden - mild enough for a gulp, honey enough to put on a sore, oil enough to anoint the smallest member (which is further defined as the little toe of a child one day old) water enough to rub off an eye-plaster, leather enough to make an amulet, ink enough to write two letters of the alphabet, coarse sand enough to cover a plasterer's trowel, reed enough to make a pen, a pebble big enough to throw at a bird, anything which weighs as much as two dried figs. The regulations continue on and on."[73]

The context by which the Scribes and the Pharisees lived by was one in which they could control. They believed they could define the context and master what was wrong and right. It is far easier to control one's actions than one's heart, so instead of having a right heart relationship with God, the Scribes and Pharisees believed that it would be sufficient to have a right action-based relationship. In an effort to define every action within the context they base their lives on, they have set themselves up for an endless task. Eventually, despite all their efforts, Jesus was the context and they were expending their lives in the wrong context.

Let's return to Israel on the way to the Promised Land and the destiny that awaits them.

The ten fearful spies that returned with a negative report were operating in the wrong context. They were not relying on the context in which God displays His power and conquers all; instead, they were working from within their finite context, which is why they had a pessimistic account of the Promised Land. This disobedience caused a whole generation of Jews to lose their inheritance because they refused to operate in God's context. There was no fear of the Lord in the people.

Years later we read about another context in the war between King Jehoshaphat against the Moabites and the Ammonites. This time, however, the context was one that incorporated the fear of the Lord. King Jehoshaphat was afraid and so he turned his attention to the Lord by proclaiming a fast. The King was wise when he determined to seek the Lord's counsel; he was setting a context for the war. He rallied and encouraged his people to have faith in God's nature of greatness:

"So Lord, the God of our fathers, art Thou not God in the heavens? And art Thou not ruler over all the kingdoms of the nations? Power and might are in Thy hand so that no one can stand against Thee."[74]

He then reminded the people of God's great deeds and what He did to overcome and bring them into the land. King Jehoshaphat finishes by saying:

"For we are powerless before this great multitude who are coming against us; nor do we know what to do, but our eyes are on Thee."[75]

God responded to King Jehoshaphat through a prophet:

"'Listen, all Judah and the inhabitants of Jerusalem and King Jehoshaphat: thus says the LORD to you, 'Do not fear or be dismayed because of this great multitude, for the battle is not yours but God's.' You need not fight in this battle; station yourselves, stand and see the salvation of the LORD on your behalf, O Judah and Jerusalem. Do not fear or be dismayed; tomorrow go out to face them, for the LORD is with you.'"[76]

Because King Jehoshaphat and his people humbled and submitted themselves to God's context, He responded to them in a powerful way and brought them success. By allowing His context to guide their lives, God was able to express Himself in the only way He can— with utter goodness and ultimate greatness.

Conclusion on Context

Context dictates every sphere of our lives: from perceptions to values, from commonplace activities to relationships. What this means is that you can't define or evaluate words or ideas and actions until you understand the context. You can't have confidence in the 'value' of a dollar until you know its worth and the reliability of the government that backs it up. Until you see your fiancé interact with his/her family, you can't fully appreciate (or not) his/her potential. It is the fear of the Lord that gives us the only true capacity to understand any situation.

"The fear of the Lord is the beginning of knowledge; Fools despise wisdom and instruction."[77]

Solomon was a wise ruler, possibly the wisest of all time. He knew how difficult it was to understand the 'timing' for each situation. He depicted his thoughts in this way:

"There is an appointed time for everything. And there is a time for every event under heaven—A time to give birth, and a time to die; A time to plant, and a time to uproot what is planted. A time to kill, and a time to heal; A time to tear down, and a time to build up. A time to weep, and a time to laugh; A time to mourn, and a time to dance. time to throw stones, and a time to gather stones; A time to embrace, and a time to shun embracing. A time to search, and a time to give up as lost; A time to keep, and a time to throw away. A time to tear apart, and a time to sew together; A time to be silent, and a time to speak. A time to love, and a time to hate; A time for war, and a time for peace."[78]

Each of these events happens within a certain context, of which dictates the timing and order the activities. The question is, who sets the context? Who ordains what happens at each time? King Solomon had the answer:

"The conclusion, when all has been heard, is: fear God and keep His commandments, because this applies to every person."[79]

The fear of the Lord will give us the context for which we should base our lives. It is the foundation for us to reach our destiny, and to glorify God. In each situation you find yourself, in each relationship you are involved with, in each job, sport or whatever the expression, unless God is invited to define the context—and your personal role in the context—there is no fear of God. Without God's context, your work will be lifeless, and it has no value in God's eyes. The fear of God is the only foundation that our work should be built on to last forever. Each of us must live our lives in the context of the presence of an Almighty God.

Chapter Seven

The Fragrance of God

Fragrance in a Putrid World

In the late 1970s there was an exodus of illegal Vietnamese refugees who fled their country in an attempt to find a place free of political and social turmoil. These "boat people," named because they risked their lives in dinky, leaky boats vulnerable to the rough South China Sea, were forced to scatter throughout South East Asia. A small number of the refugees found themselves on the shores of Hong Kong and in the jurisdiction of a confused and reluctant British government. Their newfound lives of 'freedom' weren't much better than their conditions at home. They were locked up in detention centers, surrounded by barbed wire fencing, and it was in the Whitehead Detention Center, that my friend, Janet, and her team went to serve as missionaries. As they surveyed the dismal conditions and the disrepair of the facilities, the Lord showed them they should attend to the area needing the most attention: the toilets.

These 10,000 refugees only had access to a handful of toilets that were in working order. As a result of the severely crowded conditions, most of the lavatories were overused and brimming over with excrement, flowing freely onto the floors. There was a flood of raw sewage inches deep, which served as a frenzied feeding ground for flies, maggots, and other creepy crawlies. At best, the conditions were incomprehensible, but in reality, they were inhumane.

Janet and her team got to work. They shoveled piles of excrement, unclogged the toilet bowls, fixed the flushing mechanisms, and thoroughly disinfected and cleaned the area. When she recounts her experience, she often mentions the unbearable smell of the putrefaction, indeed, at times the stench appeared to be noxious gases poisoning her system. To combat the deleterious odor, Janet would douse her clothing, specifically the inside of the elbow, with strong perfume. When the overwhelming stink was too much, she would bury her nose deep in the perfumed shirt, wrap her arm across her face, and deeply inhale the fragrant aroma to rid her nasal passages of the reek. These intermittent breaths of sweetness would encourage her that soon the task would be finished, and she would be able to leave an accomplishment behind.

Just as the fragrance allowed Janet to continue work in her desperate situation, so we as God's children should also manifest the sweet aroma of the knowledge of God everywhere we go. And like gas molecules that rise into the air and dissipate their fragrance, so our scent of hope and life should be dispersed and fall upon the people we meet, and by Brownian motion, scatter into the larger dying world.[80]

But how do we become the fragrance of God to a rancid-smelling world? It all begins with the fear of the Lord. When reverence towards God is birthed in our hearts, it will take root in our minds, and finally expressed through our collective actions.

To be God's living breath amidst a stale and complacent world we must make choices that form our destiny and reveal who God is. When our right choices are chosen consistently, these habits form the fragrance that the world eagerly inhales. Emerson once said, "what you do thunders so loudly I cannot hear what you are say," essentially, our actions give practical testimony to our faith.[81] He also said that if one fears God, "where you go, men shall think they walk in hallowed cathedrals." Men and women who truly and humbly walk in the fear of the Lord are few and far between—hence they are as precious as oxygen to the suffocating man. If our lives are filled with reverent acts, each of us will be a unique capsule producing a scented fragrance; and together we can create an interesting pot pourri of varying but complementary scents. It is only in a panorama of fragrances can we display the glorious montage that is the greatness of God's nature and character.

Even if we are consciously walking in the fear of the Lord, how can we be sure we are expressing God's fragrance to the world? By determining whether the smells of our lives contain the fragrance of reverence. Our reverent acts will create a sweet-smelling bouquet that the passerby cannot help but whiff, and be enticed.

Chapter Eight

The Fragrance of Reverence to God

Honoring People

To honor people should be a task we take delight in. The onus is not on fuss or flattery, nor does it require you to go to great lengths of effort. By a simple but genuine smile, or baking a home made apple pie for a friend, we can honor someone through acts of hospitality. When the warm, spicy fragrance of the pie tickles your friend's nose, he will feel that you've honored him. When we honor people it is an expression of acceptance in a world where we feel exiled. By actively and consciously showing affection to each other, we are being a practical testimony to God's love.[82] Acting upon our love is more important than talking about our love. In *The Ragamuffin Gospel,* Brennan Manning suggests that our religion is false if we have not love for our brethren: "Quite simply, our deep gratitude to Jesus Christ is manifested neither in being chaste, honest, sober and respectable, nor in church-going, Bible-toting, and Psalm-singing, but in our deep and delicate respect for one another."[83]

C.S. Lewis further extends the idea of honoring others: "Next to the Blessed Sacrament itself, your neighbor is the holiest object presented to your senses."[84]

We are made in God's image, and bear the responsibility of being His image bearers. No matter how different we look like to each other, no matter what shape or size, the number of appendages, or the way we sound, every existing individual bears God's image. The responsibility of this knowledge is great. Since we reflect His priceless value, each of us are individually placed in the "best" package tailored to suit us, and we are to give esteem and honor to reflect each other's preciousness. "There are no ordinary people," writes Lewis, "You have never talked to a mere mortal." And just when we overcome our guilt over this proposition, he further adds, "it is immortals whom we joke with, work with, marry, snub and exploit—immortal horrors or everlasting splendors."[85] No matter how corrupt and deformed and annoying the immortal is, please remember God is able to redeem anyone, just as He redeemed you. Mother Theresa could possibly have had the clearest and purest vision of all of us. God had given her the grace to look through the flesh, bypassing the tangible, and sensing the invaluable worth of the sick, decrepit, and dying victims on the streets of Calcutta.

It is easier to respect and give honor to those who have made right choices, specifically people who have chosen to align themselves with kingdom principles. We must treat them with respect because they model God's character. When temporarily deluded people make wrong choices and do things against kingdom principles, we must still respect them as image bearers of God, but are not obliged to respect their choices.

It is important to distinguish how we can honor those who have made wrong choices in their lives. For example:

> • A drunken father—We respect him as an image bearer of God and his parental authority. But we do not respect his choice of excess drink and the abusive actions he inflicts on those around him.
> • A homosexual—We respect him or her as an image bearer of God, but we do not honor his or her choice of a lifestyle that flagrantly flouts God's commandments.
> • An immoral president—We respect him as an image bearer of God and his position of governmental authority, but we do not have to concur with his immoral personal and public choices.

Our basic acts of reverence and honor is considered the pure scent of heaven; it is the native fragrance of paradise's ambience. We must begin exuding this scent on earth, to this end, we pray: "Your Kingdom come, your will be done on earth as it is in heaven." Reverence and honor is the crux of every relationship: the Son to the Father, the Father to the Son, the Son to His Bride (the Church), and we must see to it that the Church (His Bride) honors those the Son died to save.

Speaking Words of Life

Have you ever eaten food when you have plugged sinuses? Even genuine tasty English fish n' chips, will taste bland when our olfactory senses are not functioning properly. Just as we cannot separate our sense of taste from our capacity to smell, so the words we utter from our lips cannot be dissociated with the spiritual aroma that God detects. In *The Fragrance of Words*, Nietzsche wrote, "every word has its fragrance: there is a harmony and a disharmony of fragrance, and hence of words." The Bible says that words aptly spoken are like "apples of gold in settings of silver."[86] Our words have the power to be as sweetening as honey, as soothing as calamine to sunburned skin, and as inflammatory as a weapon. For this reason, some argue that the pen is, in fact, mightier than the sword.

Words hold great significance and power—while God spoke all creation into existence, He *breathed* human beings into existence. "Then the Lord God formed man of dust from the ground and breathed into his nostrils the breath of life; and man became a living being."[87] God's breath sustains our life, and we in turn have the opportunity to exhale His Spirit through our words onto others.

A breath is an unfinished word. When we choose to activate His breath through our will, we join with God in co-creating and verbalizing words of life. The Lord loves us and delights to have us use our creative abilities to co-create with Him. By allowing Adam to name the animals, God indicated that Adam had dominion over the animal kingdom.[88] Thoreau said "what can be expressed in words can be expressed in life." For our purposes, it would be appropriate to take this statement literally.

When our son was born, my wife and I debated back and forth for a name that would be perfect, suitable and significant. He was an expression of our love for each other, and as an expression of our love for him, we had the responsibility to define his place in the world by giving him a 'good' name. We decided on Joshua. In Hebrew, Joshua is translated to *Yeshua* and it means "Yahweh is Salvation." We still believe this name is meaningful, and both my wife and I are happy with our choice. By naming our son appropriately, we placed our blessings and hope upon him, as well as accepting our God-given parental authority over him.

Jimmy Carter made a comment about the power of words that I find interesting. Because most of us in the Western world are accustomed to the freedom of expression, we have taken for granted this liberty and failed to realize that words have the capability to inflame and catalyze change. This is his statement:

"In the life of the human spirit, words are action, much more so than many of us may realize who live in countries where freedom of expression is taken for granted. The leaders of totalitarian nations understand this very well. The proof is that words are precisely the action for which dissidents in those countries are being persecuted."

Words come from the mouth, and it is crucial to keep vigilant watch over the source of our words. The Bible repetitively stresses the importance of the tongue and the power it possesses over life and death. James is severe in his admonishments regarding the tongue: it is "a restless evil and full of deadly poison."[89] He likens the small muscle to a rudder of a boat: the rudder has the ability to turn and direct a boat, so our tongue has the ability to direct our lives, for good or for evil. The righteous can speak words that are a "fountain of life,"[90] but if a man "does not bridle his tongue…[his] religion is worthless."[91]

"The tongue is a fire, the very world of iniquity; the tongue is set among our members as that which defiles the entire body, and sets on fire the course of our life, and is set on fire by hell."[92]

In fact, James believes that if we manage to gain the self-control to restrain our tongues, we possess the ability to restrain our whole body: "For we all stumble in many ways. If anyone does not stumble in what he says, he is a perfect man, able to bridle the whole body as well."[93] This is a powerful statement and a great incentive for us to watch what we say. Jesus was stern when he heard words not uttered in truth and love:

"You brood of vipers, how can you, being evil, speak what is good? For the mouth speaks out of that which fills the heart. The good man out of his good treasure brings forth what is good; and the evil man out of his evil treasure brings forth what is evil. And I say to you, that every careless word that men shall speak, they shall render account for it in the day of judgment. For by your words you shall be justified, and by your words you shall be condemned."[94]

When we walk in the fear of the Lord, we will monitor our tongues with concerted diligence because our words reflect who God is. They are of such importance that we will be held accountable on the day of judgement for our words. We must be a people who mean what we say, say what we mean, let our yes be yes, and our no be no. We must not exaggerate, lie, bend or distort the truth, because God does not delight in a "lying tongue."[95] If we truly fear God, we will delight in using our words to extend God's kingdom here on earth, by 'naming' the world according to His desires and verbally spreading His love.

It is our choice whether our words produce the fragrance of life or the stench of death. When we choose to revere God and speak life, the aroma of peace, kindness, goodness and gentleness will produce life in others.

Giving Thanks

Although most of us have been removed from our farming roots, all cultures celebrate harvest and provision. I can still remember the woody, grassy, earthy smell of the land where I used to live. Oftentimes, in the cool shade of summer nights, and when the wind angles in the precise direction, a smell of freshly cut fields will drift into our house and linger in the air. I like to imagine that this fragrance is an enduring hint, reminiscent of the aroma in the Garden of Eden. But even if the garden did not exude this scent I would still give thanks for the aroma of fertile soil.

"The aim of life," wrote G.K. Chesterton, "is appreciation. There is no sense in not appreciating things; and there is no sense in having more of them if you have less appreciation of them." Contentment is the secret of happiness. By showing gratitude in all situations, and by attempting to find hints of goodness, rightness, and beauty in all aspects of life, we will find contentment and happiness.

The apostle Paul was well schooled in thankfulness, despite his adverse circumstances. His encouragement was "in everything give thanks; for this is God's will for you in Christ Jesus."[96] And indeed, Paul gave enthusiastic thanks in the most wretched circumstances:

"...in far more labors, in far more imprisonments, beaten times without number, often in danger of death. Five times I received from the Jews thirty-nine lashes. Three times I was beaten with rods, once I was stoned, three times I was shipwrecked, a night and a day I have spent in the deep. I have been on frequent journeys, in dangers from rivers, dangers from robbers, dangers from my countrymen, dangers from the Gentiles, dangers in the city, dangers in the wilderness, dangers on the sea, dangers among false brethren; I have been in labor and hardship, through many sleepless nights, in hunger and thirst, often without food, in cold and exposure."[97]

His evaluation of his sufferings is simple and unbelievable: "For momentary, light affliction is producing for us an eternal weight of glory far beyond all comparison."[98] Light affliction? Either Paul was made of Kryptonite, or else he had a secret that we are not aware of. His secret was this: Paul understood and accepted God's greatness and goodness, and acted upon this belief. He was convinced nothing would befall him that had not been approved by his loving Father. Therefore he considered every experience another opportunity to be God's testimony. Paul gave thanks with all his might, not for the harsh circumstances, but in spite of it, because he held onto the promise that "God causes all things to work together for good to those who love God."[99] Paul uninhibitedly praised God for His infinite wisdom and power, and in all things he behaved the way he asked the Philippians to do: "rejoice in the Lord always; again I will say, rejoice!"[100]

The world convinces us the exact opposite is true: we have nothing to be grateful for. The premise of advertising and marketing is to breed discontent and make you believe that a certain product, location, lifestyle, partner or otherwise is the answer. We are daily bombarded with advertisements, commercials, and images of what we don't have, and rightly so, because we live in reality, and the product is part of fantasy. There is only one outcome when we compare imagined fantasy and reality—reality loses out because it is not perfect. We then begin to resent reality, allowing an ideal breeding ground for feelings of envy, inadequacy, guilt, and anger. We must vigilantly guard our senses against these lies. All that glistens is not gold, rather, it is an imitation gold and the cheap covering easily peels away to reveal tarnished metal. But unless we believe that this fantasy is a façade, we will hanker for what we don't have, feel inferior, and lose our ability to appreciate. I often remind myself of a certain quote when I can't conjure up a grateful heart: "I was mad because I didn't have any shoes, until I saw the man with no feet."

Our thankfulness in every situation is not baseless or fatalistic. It is firmly rooted in God's word, which states that God is uncommonly great, and His kingdom is unshakable.

"Therefore, since we receive a kingdom which cannot be shaken, let us show gratitude, by which we may offer to God an acceptable service with reverence and awe; for our God is a consuming fire."[101]

The fire's light and heat protects us because we are in God's kingdom. When we realize that He is for us and nothing—principality, dominion, or power—can be against us, His care will engender an attitude of thanksgiving.

Paul learned to be content in all situations. How did he do this? I believe it was by a giving up his rights. In actuality, we lost all our rights to the kingdom when Adam and Eve rebelled, but often we will pretend that we have a right to rule, when we are only deceiving ourselves. We do but have one right left: the right to choose Hell. All we have to do is reject God's grace. But if we accept the grace that God freely offers, our only attitude towards Him the rest of our lives should be in prostrate thankfulness. How can we be appreciative when thieves (that's us), are adopted into God's family? Let us pray that of King Henry's request to God in William Shakespeare's play, *Henry VI* :

"O Lord that leads life, Lend me a heart replete with thankfulness!"

The fear of the Lord produces thanksgiving. Thanksgiving is a fragrant aroma in a dying world; it works like leaven because it will affect every aspect of our lives and the people around us.

Walking in Faith

Our faith, I'd like to believe, rises up as a fragrant scent to God. Some say animals can smell fear; I say heaven can smell faith. Faith is not the dull smell of old gym socks, it is the fragrant aroma of life and beauty, and directly connected to the source of life—God. Just as my friend, Janet, deeply inhaled the perfume on her clothes, so we must also relentlessly pursue the fragrance of faith, capture it, and express it admist the world's sewage.

Like the attribute of thankfulness in the previous chapter, faith is not baseless or fatalistic, nor is it, as some would believe, foolish and shallow. Faith in God is a rational, thinking step of logic, not a leap into the darkness; faith is based in reality with past events as reference points, not merely a mystical experience; nor is faith a smell of moldy traditions, it may be the sweetest scent to God.

We all have faith, but we don't all put our faith in the same things. Faith is evident in every single movement of life. Due to past experiences of solidity, you have faith that the chair underneath you will not give way; you have faith you weren't evolved from a mud puddle; you display faith when you love someone and become vulnerable; and you have a general faith in life, or else you would end your existence. For the Christian believer, our relationship with God is built on a foundation of faith, which has its roots established in God's nature and character, or, His greatness and goodness. We have faith that arising from His good nature, God created the world, and because of His great character, He maintains it. Faith is a concrete trust in God, and it is manifested in our choice to fear Him and be obedient to His guidance.

The passage in Hebrews 11:7-11 is known as the Hall of Faith, and it is an inspiring read for those of us lacking in faith.

"By faith, Noah trusted that God's awesome power could inundate and destroy the earth, so he built an ark without any visible sign of rain, much less flooding. By faith, Abram left his home and trusted that God would lead him to a place where the Lord would be the architect and builder. By faith, Sarah, Abraham's wife, trusted that God would make good on His promise, and so she conceived a child even though she was an old woman, and past the biological age of bearing children."

The list continues for those who chose to have faith in God: Moses, Rahab, Gideon, Barak, Samson, David and Samuel, only to name a few.

Here is a practical example to illustrate how our faith should be demonstrated. Imagine you are rock climbing. You intend for this climb to be short, so you only take what is necessary to last the day. At the last section, near the top of the mountain ledge, you hammer your peg into the wall and securely tie your rope around the hook. After you regain your balance and get a comfortable footing to

push off, there from above, as you are swing-
ing over the jagged rocks, a sudden grinding
metallic sound. You look up. The peg has
loosened, and it is slowly edging its way out
of the rock. You quickly lunge for the narrow
ledge that is barely in arm's reach, just as the
rope gives way and drops into the deep ravine.
A *Cliffhanger* moment. You struggle, and use
your arm muscles to pull yourself onto the
ledge. Scared and shivering, you have lost all
your equipment into the yawning mouth of the
dark crevice, and, worse still, the sun is setting
behind the horizon. You are alone.

Or so you thought. After hours of futile yell-
ing, as your voice gets hoarse and the tempera-
tures rapidly decreases, you hear a reply from
up above you. "Hello there! Is something
wrong?" Quickly and weakly, you explain the
dire situation, and the faceless voice responds,
"There is a ledge below you with a small cave
in it. You can jump drop onto it and you'll be
safe for the night."

You are not convinced of this option, because
the night is black and you can see nothing from
your vantage point. What choice do you have?
If you stay on the ledge, you will freeze to
death, but is it possible to jump into the unknown?

Here's a key question you might ask: what
kind of person does the voice belong to, and

what does he know about rock climbing? The voice tells you, "I am a professional mountain climber, and I was in your exact spot only a few weeks ago." Will this knowledge increase your trust in him? I believe it will. His wisdom and experience determines your willingness to act on his suggestion.

In the same way that you can trust the voice of the professional climber and his experience, you can trust God with your life. God knows what He is talking about, and through Jesus, He has experienced the temptations and weaknesses that you are currently undergoing:

"Therefore, He had to be made like His brethren in all things, that He might become a merciful and faithful high priest in things pertaining to God, to make propitiation for the sins of the people. For since He Himself was tempted in that which He has suffered, He is able to come to the aid of those who are tempted."[102]

Greater is our God who is in us than he who is in the world.[103] For whatever is born of God overcomes the world; we are nothing in and of ourselves.[104] In one of his self-reflections, Emerson said, "I am God in nature; I am a weed by the wall." This seeming paradox actually perfectly describes our state of being—we are but flesh, but when we are empowered by His Spirit, we can be the very expression of God. This is why faith is needed to gain the Holy

Spirit and overcome the world in victory. Faith is a shield that protects us from the fiery darts of the enemy.[105] And that which is not faith is sin.[106]

Those who are committed to walking in the fear of the Lord do so because they have internalized the knowledge of His greatness and goodness through faith. True faith cannot be divorced from fearing God any more than faith can be separated from the love of God.

Accepting Discipline and Correction

There is a visible tension evident when people strive to fulfill a task they are committed to. They are prepared to suffer to reach a certain standard of excellence or accomplishment. Winston Churchill was famous in his mental resolve, "Never give in," he said, "never, never, never, never." This dogged determination can be clearly exemplified in the world of sports. Whether in the field, the rink, the ring, the court, the course, or the water, athletes will spend hours of time and sweat buckets of perspiration to perfect their bodies for their sport. As each person strains towards his own goals, he produces a salty, pungent smell of sweat. This is the scent of self-discipline, a fragrance of the fear of God.

Sometimes I hear people discrediting Christianity as a "crutch." This is a preposterous misconception only made by people who are not aware what the mettle and pluck needed to be a committed follower of Christ. It is true that God is love and Jesus preached servitude, but this is no reason to suspect living the Christian life is easy, lazy, or otherwise. Indeed sometimes the opposite is true; we only have to look to the apostle Paul's turbulent life. Paul overcomes his situation through strict discipline and rigorous training, and an extreme motivation to win the prize in the kingdom of heaven. It is not possible to think all Christians are spineless or naïve, when one reads about Paul's aggressive, shrewd, and strategic nature:

"Do you not know that those who run in a race all run, but only one receives the prize? Run in such a way that you may win. And everyone who competes in the games exercises self-control in all things…therefore I run in such a way, as not without aim; I box in such a way, as not beating the air; but I buffet my body and make it my slave, lest possibly, after I have preached to others, I myself should be disqualified."[107]

One cannot be disciplined if one does not choose to be disciplined. It is imperative to not undermine the importance of choices. If you are struggling with a certain sin, it is not that you can not overcome it, but that you have chosen not to overcome it. The Devil may be constantly tempting you, but you must choose to constantly rebuke the Devil's schemes in

Jesus' name. In the same way, if we want to walk in the fear of the Lord, we must choose daily, even hourly, to pursue God. Unceasing meditation on King Solomon's proverbs will encourage us to follow guidelines on fearing the Lord. He says we are to treasure the Lord's commandments, make our ears attentive to wisdom, and incline our hearts to understanding.[108] It then says,

"If you seek her as silver, And search for her as for hidden treasures; Then you will discern the fear of the Lord, And discover the knowledge of God."[109]

"Because they hated knowledge, And did not choose the fear of the Lord."[110]

Notice the words "if" and "choose." The only difference between a person who follows God and a person who doesn't follow God is a decision. To believe or not to believe, this is the question, and the answer lies within us. If we are adamant about our choice, and if we exercise discipline in guarding our minds, than nothing, even death, can separate us from God's love. This is a far cry from the Christianity-crutch drivel. Fearing the Lord and following His commandments (the Moral Law) is not an abstract ideal, it can be accomplished. But as C.S. Lewis writes, "there is nothing indulgent about the Moral Law. It is as hard as nails...it does not seem to care how painful, or dangerous, or difficult it is to do. If God is like the Moral Law, then He is not soft."[111] Yet, because God is love, and He created the Moral Law, we can be sure following God's commandments will ultimately be the wisest choice to make. God will never retract his gift of free will, and will never force us to believe in Him. He longs to reveal Himself to us, but waits for us to choose Him. God told Israel to choose Him and choose life; to choose otherwise would be death.[112]

A key element in making choices is the willingness and humility to receive instruction. We can improve ourselves and hone our walk with the Lord if we are open to evaluation, criticism, and suggestions.[113] We are finite and fallible people with a limited perception, and will always have room to grow and develop. Our hearts are easily hardened in this fallen world with the deception that we can and should be self-sufficient. But really, at best, we only understand dimly.[114] Our ability to make the right choices on an ongoing basis rides to a great extent on our humility to accept wise and godly counsel. May this be our constant prayer to God—Lord, give me the serenity to accept those things I cannot change, courage to change those I can, and wisdom to know the difference.

I played a lot of sports, especially basketball, when I was growing up. I recall standing at the free throw line and shooting foul shots upon foul shots. I was determined to make the basket and would practice until I saw improvement. But improvement only comes with curbing my wrong methods, replacing them with right knowledge, and showing consistency in correct techniques. It would be futile to shoot basket after basket, hoping to improve, and all the while ignoring good suggestions and evaluations from the coach. And, the coach would also fail in his job function if he did not give me constructive feedback. In the same way, I would be an irresponsible parent if I failed to discipline and correct my son when he does something wrong.

God gave us a free will to choose options, but He also loves us too much to not reprove us when we have made wrong choices. When we choose something of lessor value over something of greater value, there are consequences as a form of punishment to correct our wrong behavior. The Bible calls this process "sanctification," and it is inextricably linked to the Father's instruction and admonishments. "Whom the Lord loves He reproves, even as a father, the son in whom he delights."[115]

Reverence indicates reference, or as mentioned earlier, it gives us a context. If we choose to revere God in our actions, we are choosing Him as the reference point for our lives. God's Word will give us feedback and evaluation, and His gentle guidance will direct us towards reality and truth. And thus, "the fear of the Lord is the instruction for wisdom."[116] Fearing the Lord will instruct us in what is true, honorable, right, pure, lovely, of good repute, and excellent.[117] And when we do these things, we are as a fragrant aroma to Him.

Authority

The modern fragrance of authority has a hint of deceit, a trace bitter foolishness, and it is overwhelmingly thick with masculine odor. This is not the original fragrance God intended leadership to be. Rather, leadership should indicate the pleasant aroma of those who walk in the fear of the Lord. All authority in the world belongs to God and he bestows power upon people who are obedient to His commandments and refuse to be tainted with a worldly smell. The original fragrance of leadership is depicted by King David:

"'He who rules over men righteously, who rules in the fear of God, is as the light of the morning when the sun rises, a morning without clouds, when the tender grass springs out of the earth, through sunshine after rain.'"[118]

The idea of authority and leadership might be an idea more difficult for the Western mind to comprehend than the Eastern educated mind. Ever since grade school, we have had

independence inculcated into us, self-suf-
ficiency stressed, and Horatio Alger exalted
because this little boy was the embodiment of
the rugged American dream. Ironically, we
have made freedom—the capacity in which all
peoples are respected to the same degree—an
oppressive religion, whereby one person's
freedom could very well impinge on another
person's freedom. We are immediately suspicious of anyone who hinders or obstructs our
independence. This perspective, in fact, is not
Biblical. The Bible clearly states that all authority is borrowed authority, and all authority
must be subject under God's authority. But we
only have to look to governmental institutions
to realize that this paradigm does not exist.
The original purpose of government was to
show God's justice and equity, but this purpose
has since become distorted and corrupted. Because of a lack of the fear of the Lord, the moral
fiber of our government has been compro-
mised and there is little hint of the fragrance
of godly justice and equanimity. Few leaders
walk out a godly life, and are motivated and
concerned with aggrandizing their own power
and wealth.

Faith is a key element to understanding and receiving God's authority. When we have faith,
we please God and He rewards the faithful.[119]
In the gospel of Matthew, we meet the Centurion who's demonstration of great faith pleases
Jesus. He understood that Jesus had sufficient

power to heal his son and was convinced Jesus had to only speak the word and a miracle would take place, and his son would be healed. He said to Jesus,

"For I, too, am a man under authority, with soldiers under me; and I say to this one, 'Go!' and he goes, and to another, 'Come!' and he comes, and to my slave, 'Do this!' and he does it."[120]

And when Jesus heard this man's words, He was amazed and pleased with his faith and understanding of the kingdom of God. The Centurion knew Jesus had complete authority under heaven and simply trusted His healing powers.

"Now when Jesus heard this, He marveled, and said to those who were following, "Truly I say to you, I have not found such great faith with anyone in Israel.'"[121]

Clearly faith in God is linked to earthly authority. Jesus, also, had to have faith in His Father, in order to withstand the political persecution in His last days on earth. His faith was greatly tested when he was brought before Pilate to be judged, but Jesus stood firm. Please bear in mind that Pilate was a godless leader. Our modern day interpretation of Pilate has at times diluted the level of his disobedience to God, and we don't consider him "such" a bad person in comparison to Jesus' more aggressive accusers. But Pilate only respected power and the fulfillment of his own desires; he is immoral and a purveyor of the oppressive government that crucified an innocent man to appease the masses. He did, however, see something different about Jesus than the average criminal:

"Pilate therefore said to Him, 'You do not speak to me? Do You not know that I have authority to release You, and I have authority to crucify You?' Jesus answered, 'You would have no authority over Me, unless it had been given you from above; for this reason he who delivered Me up to you has the greater sin.'"[122]

In the physical realm, Jesus appeared to be naïve and foolish because he entrusted himself to a godless man. But Jesus was aware that Pilate was under an infinitely bigger and divine authority—God. And so by subjecting himself to man-made authorities,[123] he was actually acting in obedience and submission to his Father in heaven. David, for example, clearly understood to never question God's authority. Although he would have liked to kill Saul, especially in defense of his own life, he understood that he had no right to remove a king—no matter how evil—if God did not allow him to. By attacking Saul, David would be indirectly attacking and undermining God's authority. From David's life we learn that unless you learn to be obedient *under* authority, you are not ready to be *in* authority.

If we are to live in a context of the fear of God then we must know that the fragrance of His authority is greater than any earthly agency we can be confronted with. Therefore, we fear the Lord by submitting to our earthly authority because all institutions carry the scent of God's heavenly authority.

Being Vulnerable

When I used to live in Asia, my wife and I would purchase our foods at the "wet market." These were open-air marketplaces where vegetables, fruits, and an assortment of live poultry and sea food—fish, shrimps, crabs and more—were for sale. When we wanted a chicken, we would select one of many feathered birds crammed into iron-wrought cages, one stacked on top of another. The vendor would pull open the cage door, grab the squawking, flapping chicken from the cluster, and tie its two legs together with vine. With dexterous movements, he grip the chicken to his side, held in place by his arm, bend its head backwards exposing the neck, and in a flash, with a quick slice of his knife, decapitate the animal. As blood gushed from the jugular vein, he would throw the headless bird in a small wooden bin situated on the floor, and let it thrash around until the blood and life slowly drained and ebbed from its body.

Grocery shopping is vastly different in America. We like our brightly lit, indoor air-conditioned warehouse, replete with clean, pre-cut, pre-packaged food, individually contained, refrigerated, and nicely wrapped in layers of cellophane. There isn't a spot of blood anywhere, and no evidence that a certain piece of meat ever belonged to a live animal. Intriguing, I thought. Do we squirm and avert our eyes when we see blood, simply because we, in the West, are not conditioned to it?

Most of my Western friends, I would venture to guess, would balk at the sight of the routine bloody massacre that happens daily in Chinese markets. The smell of blood is common to the Chinese people, as it was to the Jews of the Old Testament era. Blood—if you'll indulge my imagination—flowed freely from the pile of exposed sacrificial carcasses. A cascading fountain of thick, viscous blood would meander onto the altar, stream off the sides, and form red puddles on the sandy floor. This display of heaped raw flesh constantly reminded the Jews of the high price of atonement—calling for death to bring life. We understand now that it wasn't the blood of animals that saved them, but the blood of Jesus. We owe our lives to the shedding of Jesus' blood, and so we are called to give off the aroma of His sacrificial blood through sacrificial love. This can be expressed through living vulnerably and honestly with each other.

Love, especially the love as exemplified in the Bible, makes us vulnerable. When we love and yearn for intimacy with someone, we are essentially saying to the one we love: my happiness is linked to you, and I am incomplete without you. God made Himself vulnerable by telling us He loves us. Of course He is not "incomplete" without us, as if He lacked anything, but in a real sense, because we are created from His fingertips, he feels satisfied and "complete" with His creation around Him. As a prized possession, even as a child, if we should reject our Creator, He will feel the pain of deprivation and incompleteness. When God chose to redeem us by becoming man and divesting Himself of glory, this was His expression of ultimate vulnerability.

We will never properly walk in the fear of God until we are willing to become vulnerable and open to others. Vulnerability arises when we consciously and actively decide to give up control of our lives and let go of our preferences for the way things should be. If we have a right understanding of God's greatness and goodness, it is easier to let go of our control, because we are assured that God is too good to let us flounder, and He is too great to let anything go wrong. When we are not in control, and ask God to take control, He will guide our lives towards what is best for us. But this is terribly harder to do than to say, and everyday we must hand the reigns over to Him, and live

the day vulnerably with the understanding
that He has our best interests in mind.

The Bible tells us that God is most evident with
vulnerable people, the ones who are poor and
contrite in spirit:

"For thus says the high and exalted One who
lives forever, whose name is Holy, 'I dwell on a
high and holy place, And also with the contrite
and lowly of spirit, In order to revive the spirit
of the lowly And to revive the heart of the contrite.'"[124]

"'For My hand made all these things, thus
all these things came into being,' declares the
Lord. 'But to this one I will look, to him who is
humble and contrite of spirit, and who trem-
bles at My word.'"[125]

How do broken and contrite people live? By
giving up their wills to God, and asking Him
to break the selfishness in their lives:

- We don't have to be consumed with
  protecting ourselves, and gaining
  justice.
- We don't have to have everything the
  way we want it.
- We don't have to know everything that is
  in our future.
- We don't have to plan out everything.

- We don't have to be fully prepared, educated or financed in every opportunity we pursue.
- We don't have to pretend that we know everything.
- We don't have to win every time.
- We don't have to be "right" all the time.

There is an immense relief when we finally and permanently yield control to God and trust Him with our lives. We voluntarily empty ourselves, knowing that only as we give freely, can He fill us back up to the point of brimming abundance. We can never out-give God. Even if we were to serve Him with whole-hearted devotion, every moment for the rest of our lives, He would still deserve more because of His greatness. God desires rivers of living waters to be poured out of our lives, or, in this analogy, wondrous aromas to pour forth from our inner being. But we must have heaven residing in us in order to exude a heavenly scent. It is impossible to conjure up the scent of the Spirit, and so we must die to ourselves in order for Him to dwell on the throne of our hearts. Only at this point will the healing and forgiving aroma of sacrificial blood be the aroma our lives. We are called to be the fragrance of Christ lightly misting the world.

Walking in Obedience

For many years my wife wore the same perfume. I adored her signature fragrance. The

120

scent was as familiar to me as her voice or her face, and when she left a room, a trail of aroma would linger, hinting at the absence of her presence. When we are obedient to God and walk with Him in submission and sensitivity, we are also exerting His 'signature fragrance' and trailing it behind for people to wonder about long after our absence. There is an ongoing awareness that as we daily walk within His guidance we are giving off the aroma, but the impact is more important when we have gone, because it is the lasting impression that stays with people. They might one day, like a hound that follows a scent, trace it back to its source—our loving God. Jesus represents God's sweet distinctive signature fragrance.

Walking in the fear of the Lord produces obedience. The word "obedience" had always held negative connotations in my mind, probably a product of my legalistic background. I remember as a young man, I would often struggle to do the right thing but with no motivation behind my good deeds; I was in danger of what T.S. Eliot suggested was the worst sin—doing the right thing for the wrong motives. One day when I was in the sixth grade, as I was walking with a schoolmate home from school, I felt that I should tell him about Jesus. At church that Sunday the pastor had preached that Christians should share their faith. I didn't know how to evangelize, I wasn't even totally convinced of my own faith, but I wanted to be a good Christian and avoid hell. So not in love, but in reluctant obedience to "Christianity," I mumbled out a few words, made a jumble of it, and then tumbled along. He probably didn't make any sense either of the nonsense I was spewing.

Having struggled for many years to follow regulations and do the "right thing," I was one ordinary day struck by a gong of revelation: if I have no love, I am but a clanging cymbal to the ears of the Lord.[126] Obedience was not an issue of external compliance, but an external *manifestation* of love from within. God wants us to love Him and be vulnerable with those He calls us to love.

Obedience means a willingness to listen to instruction from someone in authority, and to act upon it immediately. I remember once I was in auto shop in high school. Our task was to tear apart a lawnmower and then to reassemble it. I didn't have a clue what to do, so I asked numerous questions, and constantly sought the teacher's help. I trusted his technical expertise and that he was willing to come to my aid. Even though my head was bent over the machinery and I was trying to figure out cog from screw and carburetor from gas tank, I was keenly aware of the whereabouts of my teacher in case I needed assistance. In the same way, we must be aware of God at all times, and boldly ask Him for help to our questions. We need His divine presence in every situation.

"My eyes are continually toward the Lord,"[127] said the Psalmist. And even in this way:

"Behold, as the eyes of servants look to the hand of their master, As the eyes of a maid to the hand of her mistress; So our eyes look to the Lord our God, Until He shall be gracious to us."[128]

If we are convinced and in awe of God's greatness, we would gladly give Him our attention and allow Him to be our authority. In any given context, we should be aware of the scent of His presence and follow it wherever it would lead us.

Finding a Vocation

The modern smell of work is drudgery and dread mixed with a squalid hint of hopelessness. The aroma of the fear of the Lord, however, is a preserving salt that retards the rancid smell of decaying life. You may catch a whiff of this reverence through a well-oiled machine or the hint of a job superbly done. Indeed when a work is done within the context of the fear of the Lord, the product will produce a heady fragrance full of hope, diligence, and zest. Just as the scent of a rose leads us to the rose, so the scent of trustworthiness and faithfulness will lead us to God's people.

We must understand that work is not a curse nor is it a result of the rebellion. Our work,

123

or vocation (the happy combination of God's intent and your talent), is an expression of our place on earth, for example, God had instructed Adam to tend to Eden before he was banished from the garden. As image bearers of God, work was intended to be a wonderful opportunity to express God's love and creativity through our will. It is only our distorted perception towards work that has now made the very word "work" laden with negative connotations.

Landa Cope, an international lecturer with Youth With a Mission (YWAM), returned "work" to its original context:

- The purpose of Man: To know God and enjoy Him forever
- Task of Man: To fill the earth and subdue it
- Strategy to fill earth: Populate nations
- Strategy to subdue earth: Various vocations

It is God's desire that all the nations of the earth will be blessed, and for the body of Christ to function in evangelism and discipleship.[129] Our vocation gives us an avenue to carry out the call to extend the kingdom of heaven on earth, and therefore, it is important for us to perform our jobs well because God does all things well.[130] We must keep in mind that we work for God and not for man. A quick test to check whether you're working with reverence to God is to ask yourself: does my work improve when my leader or boss is observing me?[131] If the answer is yes, then you trying to please man, and not God, and God should be your only audience.

We are called to be the salt of the world, and our vocation should be an expression of God working through us. Our righteous work will exude a sweet and earthy aroma that will woo the world to the presence of God.

Family

Parents are familiar with the smell of their children. From the very first moment a parent looks on the little bundle of love, each smell indelibly marks a stage in the child's life that is unforgettable. When a family functions within the context of the fear of the Lord—its members will give an aroma that leads one to think cozy thoughts of love, laughter, and a sense belonging. This poignant fragrance is memorable and will be indelibly marked on family members for the rest of their lives.

God's intention for the family was to model His father heart and allow us to understand what it means to be in God's family. Our parents should fulfill the responsibility of providing unconditional love, security, and encouragement towards the releasing of our

God-given talents. By living with our family in the beginning years of our lives, the formative years, children can observe their parents' loving and balanced relationships and be taught God's commandments for a holy living. The Bible is clear about the different roles that the husband and wife must express in their relationship. The wife is to model reverence by submitting to her husband, and the husband is to model intimacy by sacrificially loving his wife.[132] As the parents embody the Biblical model, the child will develop a clear picture of the heart of God. The child should see reverence and intimacy functioning in practical ways between his mother and father. This will develop a scent in him or her that won't be forgotten. These observations will translate it to his or her relationship with God.

God's commandment that children should obey their parents is an important one.[133] This commandment also comes with a promise: children will live long lives if they obey their parents. Why? Because they will be ready for a reverent and intimate relationship with God.

The family is a vital part of expressing the fragrance of God and preparing the next generation to know His presence. In fact, Paul writes that unless a man can successfully and righteously lead his own family, he should not lead people outside his family.[134] And if a man cannot provide sustenance for his household, then he has denied his faith and is worse than the unbeliever.[135] He is a stench and disgusting to God's nostrils. This indicates to us a normal, loving functioning family is a priority to God.

When we know the fear of the Lord we will be careful to preserve the role of the family in our lives. Whatever our role is, we should work hard to fulfill the position as best we know how so that the aromatic fragrance of God's heart will influence our family members.

From the Inside Out

The fear of the Lord begins with our realization that God sees the mind and heart of each individual, "For the ways of a man are before the eyes of the Lord, and He watches all his paths."[136] Out of an attitude of the heart, actions are birthed, but often, it is easier to control our actions than our hearts and minds.

This can be an expression of legalism, and it is a wretched smell to God. We may deceive man, but we will never deceive God. Instead of being motivated by the fear of man, we should have the fear of the Lord as our focus. When we are determined to look to God, our issues will be solved from the inside (heart), and our actions will naturally follow. "Watch over your heart with all diligence, for from it flow the springs of life."[137]

This is perhaps the most terrifying knowledge of walking in reverence before God. If it is true that our ways are ever before the Lord, then we will be judged on every conviction, thought, intention, and action. It is, in fact, much easier to focus on superficial appearances because we need to only be on guard for as long as people see us. But if you deal only with the symptoms—the action itself—and not the root that lies in your deceitful heart, then you will stay corrupted and perverted to the core. It leaves us in continual fear of being exposed, because if others get a whiff of the stench of your heart, you might be rejected.

A few years ago I went through a time period when God was dealing with some heart issues. As I was jogging along the road one morning, I saw up ahead a couple of friends walking towards me. I didn't feel like stopping in the middle of my run and talking with them, so I turned around and began to jog the other way. As I started going the other direction, I realized that I was not running away from them, but I was attempting to run away from myself. My friends served as a sore reminder of a part of myself that I didn't want to deal with. If I kept running, I would have had to stop and talk with them. If I kept running past them they might not understand. So in order to not stop and even face them I turned and ran the other way, I was too afraid of what they would think to run past them.

For the sanity and peace of our own minds, it is better to allow God to deal with our hearts according to His purpose, so we won't be continuously struggling with the same problems. If we don't allow God to shine His light into our dark places and operate on the abscess that grows in our hearts, then we will always be dodging and avoiding people who elicit things about ourselves that we don't like. The friends that I avoided did not cause my problem, rather their presence inevitably drew out my lack of self-esteem and my fear of man. As we open up a bottle of cologne, the musky, fragrant scent of the cologne will escape from the bottle. It is not the removing of the cap that causes the cologne to be inside the bottle, rather, it is the opening up that releases the fragrance of the cologne. In the same way, the hurts and inadequacies were already rife within me, but my friends opened up the cap that tightly and securely kept my shortcomings to myself. If I continued to avoid the root of my problem, then I was headed for more trouble.

Working from the inside out is not only reserved for us to deal with our own hearts, but it is also the way we should deal with other people. When I got home one day, my wife promptly informed me that Joshua, our son, had written his name in a neighbor's freshly poured concrete pad. She wanted me to deal with him.

I called Joshua to me and asked him, "I understand you wrote your name in the concrete?" He nodded that he had.

I had a sense from God to tread carefully with him on this issue. I thought for a few moments and realized that our identity was a fragrance that God put in all of our hearts. Each one of us wants our name displayed in a special, prominent place. So I asked him, "Where is our name supposed to be?"

And to my utter amazement he replied, "In the Lamb's Book of Life."

Joshua had answered correctly, though his actions should not have been as they were. But I realized that as long as his heart was in the right place, his actions would eventually align themselves appropriately as he matured over the years. "You have the right desire," I told him, "but you expressed it in the wrong way. Let's go see if we can clean up the concrete."

If I had only dealt with Joshua's action (a "bad" action or symptom), I would have crushed what was a "good" root, a God-given desire to see his name in a special place. This situation didn't require discipline but guidance. I am so thankful to God for giving me insight to work from the inside out.

Most of us, at least in our deepest hearts, believe it is enough to exhibit good behavior. And, if we are really honest with ourselves, even if we don't exhibit good behavior and do something bad, it is okay if no one knows about it. If we truly believed that every little sin will be held accountable to God, and if our God had no mercy, then we would probably all be in hell by supper. "Would not God find this out? For He knows the secrets of the heart."[138] Yes, God is extremely concerned with our actions (for faith without works is dead), but He is at any given time, more concerned with the source of our actions—our hearts.[139]

"'The heart is more deceitful than all else, and is desperately sick; Who can understand it?' 'I, the Lord, search the heart, I test the mind, even to give to each man according to his ways, according to the results of his deeds.'"[140]

When Samuel, the prophet, was searching for the next king within Jesse's sons, the Lord specifically told him that it was not any of the tall, strong, good-looking young men that Samuel thought was perfect. God warned him, "Do not look at his appearance or at the height of his stature, because I have rejected him; for God sees not as man sees, for man looks at the outward appearance, but the Lord looks at the heart."[141]

God makes it clear that He searches the heart, and He desires for it to be clean and contrite. The Psalmist prayed: "Create in me a clean heart, O God,"[142] and also, "The sacrifices of God are a broken spirit; a broken and contrite heart, O God, Thou wilt not despise."[143] He also tests men's minds and rewards each man according to his ways.[144] For God's eyes roves throughout the earth to strengthen the hearts of His children who seek Him.[145]

There is a unique, unearthly, delicate fragrance that can only originate from the heart. It cannot be imitated, manufactured, packaged in a bottle and sold to the highest bidder. Each of us can tap into the source of this heavenly scent within ourselves, and discover that each individual is as different from the next, but just as delightful. This Godly scent will not battle for an audience, because its tenderness is birthed from the spirit of a soul made in the image of God. This aromatic bouquet can only be obtained when we walk in the security of fearing God and working the way God works: from the inside out.

Hating evil

Have you ever walked into a room and, suddenly, out of nowhere, you were assaulted by an overwhelming reeking stench? Your first response is to run out the door and breathe once more. If you, however, forced yourself to stay in the room, a strange thing happens after a minute or more. In all but the worst cases, your nasal passage will equilibrate to the wretched smell and the offense gradually lessens. And if you are in the room for an even longer period, your biological systems become adjusted, so that it appears the bad smell had evaporated. When, in reality, you aren't aware that you're slowly being poisoned by the stench. Only a newcomer into the room can inform you of this fact.

It is to our detriment that we easily become normalized to the smells of the world. But we should never tolerate the stink if we adamantly walk in the fear of God. It is mutually exclusive: the fragrance of a Holy God cannot co-exist with the rotten stench of sin. If we ever lose our hatred and sensitivity to sin, then we must flee to God and ask Him to restore and heighten our awareness to the fragrance of His presence in the fear of the Lord.

I remember a conversation I once had with a non-Christian friend about another "Christian" couple who had cheated money from my friend in a business transaction. Her following comment shocked me: "It's not fair, that they [the Christian couple] can cheat and steal and still go to heaven, while I am going to hell." Her observation stirred within me a warning light—if I am to confess myself as a believer and one who walks in the fear of the Lord, I had better have moral actions to back up my life. This other "Christian" couple had chosen deception in their business and social dealings, and have become a bad testimony to a non-Christian. This is an unfortunate and awkward circumstance, especially because my friend believed the stench is directly attributed to God.

I was struck by a revelation as I was thinking about this situation. Jesus died because of His love for truth as well as His love for us. It is true that Jesus died to show God's love to the world, but this does not give us the complete picture. The complete picture is also that Jesus died in order to fulfill the truth of His words. When God told Adam and Eve not to eat the fruit because they would die, what was He to do when they had disobeyed and eaten the fruit?

If Adam and Eve lived, then God would be proved a liar. If God is a liar than He cannot be trusted and is not a good God. If He is not a good God, then we have no obligation to follow Him. On the contrary, if Adam and Eve did die, then God would lose His precious children. So how does God solve this quandary? Since God is God, after all, He finds a way out of His Catch-22.

Jesus came to fulfill the truth of God's word. God promised death, and so He would rather die (as He did through the death of Jesus) than not be true to His word. The Living Word, Jesus, came and dwelt among men to reveal God's glory.[146] His word was the light of mankind and can still be trusted today. His life restored to us a context in which to live. Isaiah shows us the foundation for Jesus' life: "And the Spirit of the Lord will rest on Him, the spirit of wisdom and understanding, the spirit of counsel and strength, the spirit of knowledge and the fear of the Lord. And He will delight in the fear of the Lord, and He will not judge by what His eyes see, nor make a decision by what His ears hear."[147]

Jesus' delight was in fearing God and living within His Father's context. Jesus looked to God as a reference point to form all his opinions and decisions, and expressed God's beauty and love through His actions. Jesus delighted living in the context of the presence of God. Jesus valued what God valued. Jesus emphasized what God emphasized. Jesus understood that fearing His Father was the foundation of all other godly attributes. He put His complete trust in God, even to the point of a painful death on the cross.

I only desire to live my life doing what God the Father shows me to do. I want God to create my context, and I no longer what to live in the fallen world's context. If God hates backbiting, jealousy, envy, stealing, strife and all expressions of selfishness, then I want to hate these things as well. Sin is stench to God, and it only leads to death. When we sin, we direct our paths towards death, and other people mistake this stench as God. No wonder people are not drawn to God, because we have failed to portray God as a living, loving Heavenly Father. We bear the onus of showing the beautiful fragrance of God to the world.

"The fear of the Lord leads to life, so that one may sleep satisfied, untouched by evil."[148]

"By lovingkindness and truth iniquity is atoned for, and by the fear of the Lord one keeps away from evil."[149]

There are no neutral smells. When we emit a smell, it communicates a message that goes straight to the heart of the world. A smell of rancorous death results from disobedience, fear of man, dishonoring others, undisciplined actions, harsh words, and otherwise. We must be careful not to dilute, compromise, or eliminate God's fragrance from this world.

Chapter Nine

An Irreverent World

I have nasal polyps that limit my ability to smell, but I was not aware of this problem until last year. Over two hundred allergies plagued me as I was growing up, and my doctor suggested that I sleep incubated in a dust free place—the bathtub. I immediately asked my mother to take me to a second opinion. Instead of a nightly porcelain tomb, I opted to take weekly allergy shots. After a while, these inoculations became a tiresome and time-consuming routine, and so I altogether stopped going to the doctor's office. Needless to say, my capacity to smell is limited and my taste buds are unrefined in comparison to the average person. But I would not have known my deficiency had the doctor not informed me of my polyps. Ignorance was bliss; now I feel jipped when others rave about a scrumptious meal or a delicious smell—I cannot heighten my senses and enjoy the same pleasure. In a very real sense, my severely diminished sensitivity to taste and smell is like the world's diminished sensitivity to God's fragrance. Allow me to use this lack of sensitivity as a metaphor for an irreverent world.

Imagine walking into a large meat market and noticing something amiss, but you are unable to put your finger on the problem. As you look around at the different shaped and sized meat slabs, you begin to question the price tags. The costs were all wrong, or rather, the value attached to a particular piece of meat was wrong. A chicken foot sold for three times the price of chicken breast? The price of pig toenails—pig toenails— the same as the cost of veal? That's what's wrong: the price tags are mislabeled and so is—you begin to sniff the air—the overpowering pungent smell. The odor is suspicious. It stinks like rotten meat and you are surprised that you didn't notice this anomaly earlier. The other shoppers are oblivious to your revelation and continue to unsuspectingly choose decomposed, possibly poisonous, meat. You try telling your fellow shoppers about the incongruous pricing and the decaying meat, but they all push their shopping carts around you, thinking you must be the town square loony. Instead of thanking you for your concern, they edge away from you. You hope you are in a bad dream, and that this painful situation soon ends.

As outlandish as this scenario sounds, this is how the Bible describes our world. Our value system has gone haywire: it is a place where rotten meat is lauded and in high demand, and what should be prized is demeaned and ignored. Distressingly, the majority of the world does not realize that they are deceived because they are born into a false system of values. They are left blinded until God's enlightenment shows them there is a different standard.

Media, all types including television, radio, film, computers, and otherwise, provoke and preserve the scent of the world, especially for Western youth. It is estimated that the average American child is exposed to thousands of beer commercials by the time he is 21—at which time he will be old enough to order his own alcohol. Another study, by the Kaiser Family Foundation, found that the typical American child spends more than 38 hours a week as a "media consumer" in a home that averages three TVs, three tape players, two VCRs, two CD players, a video game player and a computer. The ceaseless bombardment of advertisements serves as brainwash. We are convinced that these images represent reality, and they portray what we are to look like, to wear, to eat, to live, and other ideas. Marketers are not naïve, they know it is difficult to sell a product based directly on the product's qualities because the consumer will have a binary choice. They can either reject or accept the product on the basis of knowledge, need, and pricing. Instead, they will portray and link the product to an attractive and desirous lifestyle of the target market segment. By purchasing a Virginia Slims cigarette, say, advertisers are selling the lifestyle of the women who supposedly smoke Virginia Slims—happy, carefree, and their stick thin legs are dressed in Capri pants perfect for the yachting trip. The cigarette becomes part and parcel of the image, and the consumer buys the product, subconsciously hoping to purchase the lifestyle as well.

A farce is exposed when we objectively unpack the advertiser's ploy. Most people will agree it is impossible to "buy" a lifestyle. But tell this to advertisers who continue to dupe their consumers; tell this to consumers, who, when they see the sexy, bikini-clad woman perched on a product, will buy the washing machine. The washing machine obviously does come with "white," "colors," and "woman" buttons but advertisers know that "sex sells," and so we will find beautiful women in advertisements ranging from furniture to stationary sets.

Why have I belabored this point? Because I am trying to expose a deception we get easily entangled in. The world tells us that laughter, contentment, peace, and affirmation can be sold in a bottle, as readily available as cheap fragrance. But these scents are only temporary and should not be confused with the reality of God's presence and the priceless aroma He emits through His children. Indeed pleasures, artificial pleasures, can be, like preservatives, sustained, however, we all agree that Wal-Mart strawberry jam can never taste better than natural, home-made strawberry jam. The pure and untreated scent of a rose can never be reproduced by a machine, and even if it could, the bottle could not compare to the exquisite perfection of a real rose. Artificial, perfect imitation products can never substitute genuine goods. Just ask your wife if she would want—price not withstanding—an excellent quality cubic zirconium or a diamond ring. Just as her answer would indicate that "diamonds are a girl's best friend," so should our certainty when we compare God's aroma to the faint scents of this world. But if our nostrils have been inundated with the world's smells, we will adjust to this fragrance and accept this version of life.

When we are finally offered a whiff of the pure, sweet scent of God, we will snap to our senses like the prodigal son. But by that time, our olfactory nerves will have been damaged. We need to humbly ask God to forgive our ignorance, and restore a proper understanding within us. When we ask the Lord to transform our minds, we bring the tangible world back into the heavenly kingdom. This is no small step that we are taking. When we change loyalties, we are pledging to no longer:

- Be conformed to this world. "And do not be conformed to this world, but be transformed by the renewing of your mind."[150]

- Find our value in the world. "But may it never be that I should boast, except in the cross of our Lord Jesus Christ."[151]
- Be taken captive to the world's principles. "See to it that no one takes you captive through philosophy and empty deception, according to the tradition of men...rather than according to Christ."[152]
- Be stained by the world. "This is pure and undefiled religion in the sight of our God and Father...to keep oneself unstained by the world."[153]
- Love the world or the things of the world because then the Father's love can not be in us. "Do not love the world, nor the things in the world. If anyone loves the world, the love of the Father is not in him."[154]

God is unequivocal in His challenge, we are to choose Him over the world. And hopefully we will, like Joshua, choose to serve God wholeheartedly: "...but as for me [Joshua] and my house, we will serve the Lord."[155] Joshua was aware that the Lord would tolerate no less devotion than our entire beings, and so he encouraged the Israelites to "cling"[156] (adhere, stay, remain in) to the Lord.

When we have chosen to revere the Lord as God, it will do well to understand what we have rejected. We have chosen to discard the irreverent world, a place where reverence and faith are placed in objects, people, or institutions that are not worthy of such esteem. God made us in His image, and placed in us a yearning for something sublime and greater than our petty, ephemeral lives. This is a God-sized and God-shaped hole that only God can fill. But if we do not realize that only He can meet our desires, then we will end up desperate and frustrated, trying to find unworthy things to fulfill us. This is irreverence. True reverence is a response to reality; irreverence is a wrongly placed reaction to deception and fantasy, the figment of our imaginations. An example of irreverence is when I valued my silver Jaguar more than I should have. At basic level, the Jaguar was only an aesthetically pleasing car, but my esteem for the metal machine was beyond its worth. I even let the car speak of my worth as a human being. This is an irreverence of the worst degree. As I have established earlier, only Jesus dying for our sins speaks of our priceless value. I am worth more than ten Jaguars, and to not acknowledge this fact would be to belittle God and His sacrificial love through Jesus Christ.

The world will try to distract us with a variety of cheap, imitation fragrances. Let us look at some of these in turn.

Fear of Man

When we live for the fear of man, we are living for kudos in men's eyes, their audience, and their applause. This is when we live for the desire to see men, and to be seen by them. Praise and adulation is an addictive scent, but its quality denotes cheap plastic. At first its fragrance is refreshingly buoyant, but it quickly evaporates and disintegrates into thin air, which is why there never seems enough of it.

Unless we realize that men's praise are as fleeting as men themselves, we will continue to judge ourselves by the way other people define us. Value, said British economist W. Stanley Jevons, is the most "impalpable of ghosts." "[Value] will come and go unthought of while the visible and dense matter remains as it was." For a person who's occupation deals with monetary values and its consistently fluctuating patterns, we should believe Jevons's words. No matter how much praise we get, or how much we lack, the "visible and dense matter," that is, our bodies and the spirit and soul, will remain as it was. In God's eyes, we do not become more valuable when we have achieved the million-dollar mark, nor do we decrease in value when we are crippled and unable to work. God's context is permanent and dependable while man's glory is limited and fickle. Jesus was clear about this when he states, "I do not receive glory from man."[157]

Though the world will loudly try to dictate the context for your life, and delineate what is meaningful, successful, and try to define happiness, be on your guard and expose these fallacies as lies. One must constantly and actively undermine the world's standards as a cheap imitation fragrance of God's holy standards.

Before our family returned to Oregon in 1988, I occupied the position of directorship in a Singapore YWAM ministry for five years. It was difficult returning to Salem where no one cared about my accomplishments, nor did they "revere" me in the way I felt that I deserved. In Singapore, I was deferred to and given preferential treatment; in Salem, I only elicited strange looks when I told neighbors I was a missionary. To them, being a missionary was, at best, a "different" occupation, at worst, they avoided me like one would avoid a guilty conscience. I struggled with feelings of inferiority and went into slight depression. I should have known better; but I had begun to believe in the world's value system, and was ashamed that I scored so low in its valuation. I should have realized that my value lies within myself, not without. "The whole value of the dime is in knowing what to do with it," said Emerson. The value of the dime is ten cents, and it will always be ten cents. I might be able to purchase less for ten cents now, due to inflation, than I was able to purchase twenty years ago, but the dime is still, in numerical value, ten cents. Through investments—intelligent, bullish, or foolhardy—I might be able to increase or decrease the ten cents. In the same way, my "numerical" value in Salem and Singapore is exactly the same, and my core worth will never change no matter what my situation is.

More recently, I was relieved to have finished my doctoral degree. I clearly knew that God had directed me to do my PhD, even though I had been initially reluctant to pursue additional educational endeavors. After laboring arduously for seven years, as a result of my efforts, I wanted to take the credit and title of "Doctor Rawlins." But I struggled with this introduction considerably. My flesh screamed for recognition, but my spirit constantly reprimanded me for finding value in a certificate. Ironically, my PhD brought me more headaches and heartaches than I bargained for. If I accepted the lie that I was more valuable because of my degree, I would reek a foul smell to God, and that was the last thing I wanted. Finally, I relinquished control of my doctorate to God. The tension between humility and vanity was too heavy for me to bear, and I promised the Lord that I would look to my degree no longer. Since I have made this decision, I have found a liberating mental freedom to be myself and not be caught up in the world's system. If I am given to boast, my only boast should be in what the Lord has done for me.[158]

King Saul was also an unfortunate victim of the world's values, and by honoring men's opinion more than he valued God's estimation, he alienated the Lord and lost his destiny. God had commanded Saul to thoroughly destroy the evil Amalekites because of their repugnant actions; they would sneak up on Israel's pregnant women and cut open their stomachs, and they were rife with diseases. God decided that Saul was to be His instrument of judgement against the Amalekites. But Saul did not obey God because he feared man more than he feared God. He kept the best livestock alive and also preserved the life of the Amalekite king. When King Saul was confronted by Samuel, he replied:

"I have sinned; I have indeed transgressed the command of the Lord and your words, because I feared the people and listened to their voice. Now therefore, please pardon my sin and return with me, that I may worship the Lord." But Samuel said to Saul, "I will not return with you; for you have rejected the word of the Lord, and the Lord has rejected you from being king over Israel."[159]

Even during a critical moment of Saul's judgement, the King was still concerned with being honored before his people. His fear of man had caused him his kingdom and, ironically, an infamous reputation in history.

"And as Samuel turned to go, Saul seized the edge of his robe, and it tore. So Samuel said to him, 'The Lord has torn the kingdom of Israel from you today, and has given it to your neighbor who is better than you. And also the Glory of Israel will not lie or change His mind; for He is not a man that He should change His mind.' Then he said, 'I have sinned; but please honor me now before the elders of my people and before Israel, and go back with me, that I may worship the Lord your God.'"[160]

Saul was a stench in God's nostril because he lusted for men's approval. He lived in an irreverent world where the context was formed by people's opinion. These opinions are only arbitrary values. If you strive for this earthly "goal," I promise that soon you will feel vacuous and frustrated. "Vanity of vanities!" decries King Solomon, "all is vanity."[161] Even back in the 1800s, Emerson forewarns us that conformity to the majority will not bring happiness, instead, at the end, our consciences will get the better of us.

"You must pay for conformity. All goes well as long as you run with conformists. But you, who are honest men in other particulars, know, that there is alive somewhere a man whose honesty reaches to this point also, that he shall not kneel to false gods, and, on the day when you meet him, you sink into the class of counterfeits."

God asks Israel why they should fear men:

"Who are you that you are afraid of man who dies, and of the son of man who is made like grass; That you have forgotten the Lord your Maker, who stretched out the heavens, and laid the foundations of the earth."[162]

God's children had lost their reverence for Him and become consumed with reverence for other men. This struggle is not individual to Israel, every person in every generation struggles between fear of man and fear of the Lord. Jesus confronted the religious leaders of His day. More than anyone else, these spiritual authorities should have known better than to regard the opinion of men and not God. Jesus said of them:

"You are those who justify yourselves in the sight of men, but God knows your hearts; for that which is highly esteemed among men is detestable in the sight of God."[163]

"And when you pray, you are not to be as the hypocrites; for they love to stand and pray in the synagogues and on the street corners, in order to be seen by men. Truly I say to you, they have their reward in full."[164]

"But they do all their deeds to be noticed by men; for they broaden their phylacteries, and lengthen the tassels of their garments."[165]

"Woe to you, Scribes and Pharisees, hypocrites!
For you are like whitewashed tombs which on
the outside appear beautiful, but inside they
are full of dead men's bones and all uncleanness."[166]

What do you think a "dead men's bones and
uncleanness," would smell like? Putrid. And
this is the disgusting smell that God wrinkles
His nose at when we fear men more than we
fear Him. We would be emitting a deathly
fragrance and be at odds with God.

Religion

Sometimes instead of revering men, we will
revere gods of the spirit world. The premise of
many religions, especially Eastern religions, is
to live in such a way as to appease the spirits
and earn their favor. If they are pleased with
you, blessings will fall upon you and your family; if they are not pleased with you, then you
can be certain that misfortune is headed your
way. If you are a Hindu Indian, you will perform acts to please your one million or so gods.
If you are a Chinese Buddhist, you will burn
incense as a sign of reverence to your ances-
tors.

But if you are reading this book, you are probably not concerned with rat gods, zen, or
Nirvana. Instead, your burden is that of the
"good Christian"; going to church on Sunday,

being pious, and denying your gut instinct to despise your neighbor. The struggle for most of us Western Christians is organized, legalistic religion. In the previous chapter I had mentioned legalism in the section "From the Inside Out." My thesis still stands: if we reverence men and the "spirit" of denominational Christianity more than God, than our actions will be derived from the outside and not initiated from our hearts. If we are not careful to examine and wipe the lenses by which we see the world, then our vision will be marred with the filters of our denomination, prejudices, traditions and otherwise.

If at any time institutionalized religion bears a greater influence than the presence of God, this event hails the beginning of the end. Past experiences should be honored and traditions remembered, but what went before cannot always be applied to current situation. Change happens inevitably, and Christianity should be made applicable to the times. The Israelites were careful to observe their works, but to the expense of understanding the significance behind their actions.

"…Because this people draw near with their words and honor Me with their lip service, but they remove their hearts far from Me, and their reverence for Me consists of tradition learned by rote…"[167]

It is easy to damage our witness by tainting it with conformity rather than unity. Conformity, as in Emerson's illustration above, is contrasted with honesty. Thus conformists are not honest; they are dishonest regarding their intentions, their feelings, and their relationship with God. They think they are spiritual and close to God when, in actuality, they are only performing rites and following regulations. Oscar Wilde warns us against superficiality in his usual flippant, but enlightening manner: "it is only the superficial qualities that last. Man's deeper nature is soon found out." Unity on the other hand, is when individual diversity is encouraged and expressed in a unified way. Unity flourishes in love; the world will know we follow Christ by evidence of our love and unity.[168] When we lose our unique bouquet of mixed aromas, then we will smell as this world does, replete with a range of cacophonous smells.

Signs of life killing conformity can be found in the following scenarios:

- We do what others expect rather than what is right.
- We cling to the illusion that a group is invulnerable.
- The group's will becomes the moral standard for what is right.
- Peer pressure is used to silence deviant questions or doubts.

- Any communication that discredits the group is silenced.
- Communication is created or censored to meet the needs of the group.

When conformity replaces unity we lose the sense or desire for the beautiful aroma of God's presence. It is easier to ride on inertia and the success of past experiences than to venture and risk hearing God's message for today. This cowardice and dishonesty is a rancid smell to God. The Pharisees and Sadducees are perfect examples of superficial know-how and inner vacuity.

Traditions are important and have much to teach us. But we must always identify the underlying principle of tradition, and understand what it reveals about God. If we place our value in traditions as a form of identity, and do not attempt to apply the principles to our lives, then we are only stinky fools in God's eyes.

Pride

The most vulgar and repulsive stench to God is pride. As the most humble being in the universe, God is disgusted with an expression contrary to Himself. Pride is irreverent in its self-reverence; and when one is consumed by oneself, one cannot be in awe of God. And God is a jealous, consuming fire that wants our entire being.[169] Pride could be construed as the foundation for all irreverence because it is the source of the fetid stench. Pride is the root of self-centeredness, self-exaltation, self-righteousness, self-glorification and other forms of self-deception. C.S. Lewis poignantly describes our struggle with pride:

"There is one vice of which no man in the world is free; which every one in the world loathes when he sees it in someone else; and of which hardly any people, except Christians, ever imagine that they are guilty themselves. I have heard people admit that they are bad-tempered, or that they cannot keep their heads about girls or drink, or even that they are cowards. I do not think I have ever heard anyone who was not a Christian accuse himself of this vice. And at the same time I have very seldom met anyone, who was not a Christian, who showed the slightest mercy to it in others. There is no fault which makes a man more unpopular, and no fault which we are more unconscious of in ourselves. And the more we have it ourselves, the more we dislike it in others.... The essential vice, the utmost evil, is Pride.

Unchastity, anger, greed, drunkenness, and all that, are mere fleabites in comparison: it was through Pride that the devil became the devil: Pride leads to every other vice: it is the complete anti-God state of mind."[170]

The Psalmist wrote:

"In his pride the wicked does not seek him; in all his thoughts there is no room for God." [171]

C. S. Lewis continues with his exposition of pride:

"Each person's pride is in competition with every one else's pride. Two of a trade never agree. Pride is essentially competitive—by it's very nature—while other vices are competitive only, so to speak, by accident. Pride gets not pleasure out of having something, only out of having more of it than the next man. We say that people are proud of being rich, or clever, or good-looking, but they are not. They are proud of being richer, or cleverer, or better-looking than others. If every one else became equally rich, or clever, or good-looking there would be nothing to be proud about. It is the comparison that makes you proud: the pleasure of being above the rest.

"Power is what pride really enjoys: there is nothing makes a man feel so superior to others as being able to move them about like toy soldiers. If I am a proud man, then, as long as there is one man in the whole world more powerful, or richer, or cleverer than I, he is my rival and my enemy. In God you come up against something which is in every respect immeasurably superior to yourself. Unless you know God as that—and, therefore, know yourself as nothing in comparison—you do not know God at all. As long as you are proud you cannot know God."[172]

Pride loves and seeks power. Power will allow a person to "be god" and define the context of his own life and the life of others. Pride hates and rejects vulnerability. Pride cannot stand visible signs of weakness or fallibility. The stench of irreverence is strongest when people refuse to admit their limitations even though they are mistaken. This is the very work of Satan, and we see evidence of his work when he deceives Adam and Eve into thinking they could be like God, knowledgeable in good and evil. Satan tried to set a false context for their lives. Only God the Creator should set the context of our lives.

Pride results in the sin of self-exaltation.[173] This exaltation lifts up ourselves to a position of authority, value, and the power to define the context of our lives. In fact, an over-simplistic but truthful answer for war, strife and struggle lies in self-exaltation. It is when one's pride fights against another one's pride. Each person wants to define the context for his life without outside interference. The Bible is clear about the stench of pride:

"Everyone who is proud in heart is an abomination to the Lord; assuredly, he will not be unpunished."[174]

Anytime I believe that I can, and should, define the context for my life ("take charge, Matt, I tell myself"), I tread very cautiously. One must be forewarned when he attempts to walk against the Lord. But my pride is more foolhardy than wise, and sometimes I find myself at odds with all the power and resources available to Heaven.[175] When I choose to govern myself, I will emit a repulsive stench to God. We are assured that our Sovereign God will punish any irreverent individual who promotes the 'self' instead of God.

Chapter Ten

Is Reverence Enough?

The active volcanoes of the Big Island are one
of the of the biggest tourist attractions in Hawaii. Tens of thousands of visitors flock to
Kailua-Kona and drive two hours to see the
slow flow of the bright orange, molten lava
meandering its way through the lava crevices,
building layers upon layers, drying into sedi-
mentary-like rock slabs. The most spectacular
place to watch this spectacle, in my opinion, is
at the edge of the cliff where the lava flows and
falls into the Pacific Ocean. When the searing
heat of the volcanic emission meets the cool
ocean, the hiss and fume and intense smell of
sulphur is overwhelming. Another place that
tourists like to visit is Mauna Kea, the island's
tallest and grandest peak. On cloudless nights,
it is possible for stars to completely brighten
the sky whereby the "night" sky is fully illuminated with specks of black, instead of a dark
sky with spots of starlight. And if this display
of greatness was unsatisfactory, one could
make use of the super powered telescope that
probes deeply into the heavens and observes
the universe in detail. This scintillating dem-

onstration of the galaxy's immensity should be enough to make the proudest person bow.

But for those who do not believe that in a Creator and His divine plan, this brilliance is nothing more than a breathtaking vision that is devoid of significance. This emptiness is regrettable, and may lead to a slight feeling of desperation. This is the way one scientist describes the vastness of the universe:

"As a result of the gradual shift in our understanding of ourselves and our universe, humanity now appears to be a tiny living system inhabiting a speck of cosmic dust that orbits a mediocre star about two-thirds of the way out from the center on one arm of one galaxy somewhere in an expanding universe of numberless galaxies.

"From this perspective, we are not the center of the universe in any terms, and our existence is of no measurable consequence to cosmic processes. This shift in models continues to produce a variety of reactions in human psychic systems. One could well conclude that humanity is of no consequence in the universe."[176]

Reverence for God and His creation is not enough for an intimate relationship with Him. As Kant mentioned earlier, fear—the types that alludes to reverence of the Sublime—makes us feel weak and vulnerable. If there is no other feeling towards God but fear and reverence, then He will be nothing than an unfamiliar, impersonal, spiritual deity sitting in the great big sky.

The Israelites feared the Lord and served Him according to their customs.[177] Their reverence for God was not based on His being the one and only God, nor was it based on love, but on a fear of retribution and hell. For this reason, they easily turn away to idolatry. Reverence alone is not enough to keep us enraptured and besotted with God. Even the demons reverence and "shudder"[178] at God because they are terrified of His greatness and awesome power. Yet His supremacy does not engender love in the demons, instead their pride and jealousy increases all the more and they continue to rebel.

There must be something more than reverence and fear of the Lord that secures us to Him.

At the beginning of this book I mentioned that truth has two wings. Reverence towards God's greatness is only one wing of the truth. The other wing of truth is God's character of love. We need both wings to soar into the heavens with God.

Chapter Eleven

Character of God

Love

Over arching all theological knowledge, we
must internalize that God is Love.[179] To God,
"love" is a noun, not only a verb. He loves
and embodies Love. Love loves to love, and so
Love creates more human beings to love. This
is the reason why God created human beings
in the first place: in order to give His love to
us. Throughout this book we have not concen-
trated so much on God's love, but on His greatness. The greater He is the more love He has,
and so we relate to Him through His power.
But God does not relate to us through His
power, but through His love. He primary mo-
tive in bringing us forth from dust was not to
worship Him, but He created us to enjoy Him
and to receive His love. Therefore our primary
responsibility is to receive His love and then to
respond to Him with our hearts. When Adam
and Eve sinned and fell out of an intimate relationship with Him, God demonstrated His love
in this way: while we were still sinners, He
sent His son to die in order to redeem us back
to heaven.[180]

All of God's choices are made in the context of His love, even responses that don't seem lovely, such as discipline, wrath, and jealousy, are only a by product of His love. Initially, it is important to have a fear of His greatness, because then we can *all* the more appreciate His encompassing, enveloping love. Paul understood God's love was unending:

"Who shall separate us from the love of Christ? Shall tribulation, or distress, or persecution, or famine, or nakedness, or peril, or sword? Just as it is written, 'For Thy sake we are being put to death all day long; we were considered as sheep to be slaughtered.' But in all these things we overwhelmingly conquer through Him who loved us. For I am convinced that neither death, nor life, nor angels, nor principalities, nor things present, nor things to come, nor powers, nor height, nor depth, nor any other created thing, shall be able to separate us from the love of God, which is in Christ Jesus our Lord."[181]

It is imperative to thoroughly grasp an understanding of God's love. Once God graces us with this revelation, nothing, absolutely nothing, can deter our feverish devotion to the Almighty. And when this revelation comes, we will express Romans 14:7-8 with as much certainty and simplicity as stating our name:

"For not one of us lives for himself, and not one dies for himself; for if we live, we live for the Lord, or if we die, we die for the Lord; therefore if we live or die, we are the Lord's."[182]

When we see the beauty of His love through His greatness, we will be breathless and awed. With happiness, we will realize that the fear of the Lord is inextricably linked to the love of the Lord.

"For as high as the heavens are above the earth, so great is His lovingkindness toward those who fear Him."[183]

"Oh let those who fear the Lord say, 'His lovingkindness is everlasting.'"[184]

"Behold, the eye of the Lord is on those who fear Him, on those who hope for His lovingkindness"[185]

Righteousness

God knows what is right because of His greatness; God loves what is right because of His goodness. The only benchmark for righteousness is based on God's standards. Israel did not know God's righteousness so they were unable to act righteously:

"For not knowing about God's righteousness, and seeking to establish their own, they did not subject themselves to the righteousness of God."[186]

If God's nature is the only standard for righteousness, then as certain as the Law exists, so is our own failure to keep the Law. God lovingly and sacrificially sent His son to pay for the penalty of our sin for failing to keep the Law, not, as some would have to believe, to abolish the Law itself. Jesus' death on the cross was a fulfillment of the Law, and within this golden nugget of truth lies the very power of God's gospel:

"For I am not ashamed of the gospel, for it is the power of God for salvation. For in it the righteousness of God is revealed."[187]

Following God's law in a fallen world may seem at times to be an arduous, inconvenient, dangerous, and excruciating task. Nevertheless we are created and called to holy, because God is holy, and therefore in faith, we are committed to follow His Law of Love. One must take heart and remember that the pain of following the Law of love is only "momentary affliction." Something greater is in store for us, and that is His love and reward. If the Law is from God, and God is Love, then the Law must have its roots in Love.

"Listen to Me, you who know righteousness, a people in whose heart is My law; do not fear the reproach of man, neither be dismayed at their revilings."[188]

"But for you who fear My name the sun of righteousness will rise with healing in its wings; and you will go forth and skip about like calves from the stall."[189]

"..but in every nation the man who fears Him and does what is right, is welcome to Him."[190]

"Who will not fear, O Lord, and glorify Thy name? For Thou alone art holy; for all the nations will come and worship before Thee, For Thy righteous acts have been revealed."[191]

Holiness

God's holiness is like a pervading aura of shimmering white light. This radiance is strong and pure, but at the same time warmly embracing. As fireflies draw towards a flickering candle, so God's children will be drawn into His holiness. Anything unholy repels away from God's holy light. God created the ideal context for our lives and will not for one moment pretend His perspective is other than perfect. He loves us, even in our broken state, but He loves us too much to let us stay as we are. Therefore, if we allow Him to guide us, He will gently but firmly lead us to enlightenment and a fuller understanding of His wisdom and greatness. When we are intimately acquainted with His nature, we will naturally desire to draw from His context of life. We will inevitably move towards holiness. We know we have the fear of the Lord upon us if we move perceptibly closer towards God's impeccable standard of holiness.

"Therefore, having these promises, beloved, let us cleanse ourselves from all defilement of flesh and spirit, perfecting holiness in the fear of God. God is light and in Him there is not darkness."[192]

We should have no illusions or cling to any deceptions regarding God's tolerance for sin. He has none. God is holy and can only reveal Himself as He is. If we want to intimately know Him, we can only know Him through holiness. When we see His holiness and begin to walk in it, our lives will affect our family, our neighbors, and even nations.

"And I will vindicate the holiness of My great name which has been profaned among the nations, which you have profaned in their midst. Then the nations will know that I am the Lord," declares the Lord God, "when I prove Myself holy among you in their sight."[193]

If we do not choose to walk in His holiness, then we can expect His discipline in our lives:

"For they [our fathers] disciplined us for a short time as seemed best to them, but He disciplines us for our good, that we may share His holiness."[194]

Humility

God is opposed to the proud and gives grace
to the humble because He is humble. God is
also secure in His strength because He has all
authority, and He does not get threatened or
power hungry like earthly rulers. Govern-
ments will war against each other to gain or
maintain status, but God is awesome and
powerful and does not need to prove His
strength. In fact, He set aside His heavenly
crown in order to come to the world He created
to redeem us. Here is the amazing paradox:
in all of God's unsearchable greatness, He also
desires to be intimately personal with each of
us. Not even our mother or husband can know
the number of hairs on our heads, such as God
does.

"The Lord is high above all nations; His glory
is above the heavens. Who is like the Lord our
God, who is enthroned on high, who humbles
Himself to behold, the things that are in heaven
and in the earth?"[195]

If God had any hint of pride He would not
have divested Himself of power and taken on
the form of a man. Not just a man, but a common servant, unattractive, born in a bare barn,
and died on a wooden cross. But to effectively
reveal His heart to us, He had to die a humble
death.

The Bible tells us that the fear of the Lord is the beginning of wisdom, and that wisdom is with the humble. Therefore we can ascertain that the fear of the Lord and humility are inextricable.

"The reward of humility and the fear of the Lord, Are riches, honor and life." [196]

Grace

Grace is getting what we don't deserve. All of us have had the occasion to feel that we do not warrant something. But not often, I would venture to guess, do we feel utterly undeserving. The key to unlocking the exquisite joy of the true worth of grace is to understand we can never justify deserving God's grace.

Let me draw some examples. If Celia and I had kept the Jaguar permanently, I would have felt that, being a missionary, and living on financial support from family and friends, I didn't deserve a car like the Jaguar. In fact, I probably would have felt compelled to sell the car for missions outreach money or offered the money to someone else. My mentality would be different if I worked at a thriving multinational company. If I had been a longstanding employee, constantly putting in eighty hours a week, and shouldering the responsibility of Chief Financial Officer, I would feel that I deserved a Jaguar. I am justified for owning this luxury car, I would tell myself, I am worthy enough to own this car.

Or, sometimes we might get an undeserved compliment. But because we feel that we didn't do a great job, or because we didn't put in as much effort as we should have, or because the glory came too easily—we feel that we don't deserve the gracious compliment. But if we had performed splendidly, spent days in preparation, and worked our tails off, then the compliment is deserved, and we might even hanker for more. Or, what if a neighbor you hardly knew, and actually quite disliked, spent hours baking the most delicious, most cinnamon-tasting apple pie for your family? You would be embarrassed by the act of hospitality, and feel that you didn't deserve the delicious pie.

Say you felt undeserving in all these scenarios. But if you had worked harder, were nicer, or did better, these efforts would deserve the compliments, gifts and rewards. If I ever feel undeserving of something, I could usually define an action that would make me more deserving of it. If I had been kinder to my neighbor, and she baked me an apple pie, then I would feel that I earned the pie.

This is not the case with grace. No matter how hard we work, how nice we are, or gracious our attitudes, we will never deserve God's mercy. Mercy is not getting what we deserve, in this case, eternal death in hell's cauldron. Nothing could ever justify the King of kings and Lord of lords, our Heavenly Father, and Creator of the Universe from leaving heaven in order to become a common man and die a criminal's death to redeem us from hell.

With this knowledge in mind, we should therefore abdicate any intentions we've had to earn God's grace and mercy. We cannot gain more grace and mercy, and there is no option of God's grace and mercy decreasing. God is Love, and because of His great love towards us, He offers us mercy, forgiveness, and sanctification so that we can join Him in heaven.

Although God is always offering us His mercy and grace, we cannot receive it unless it is with faith and obedience. As we have learnt, faith and obedience are a result of the fear of the Lord. Only those that fear Him will receive His mercy and grace:

"And His mercy is upon generation after generation toward those who fear Him."[197]

God imparts mercy to those who fear Him not because He is stingy, but because those who fear the Lord will not abuse His free gift. God's mercy is free for us, but it cost God His son's life. When we do not possess a healthy fear of God, then after receiving His grace, we may turn against His gift and mock Him by irreverence.

Judicious

God is the guardian of all truth. It is the position that His greatness and goodness requires Him to take. He is the one to set the universal standard: whom He approves will live forever and whom or what He disregards will die an eternal death. God is merciful, He possesses a father's heart that reaches out to each of His children. But when our Father steps into the role of Judge, He will impartially judge the whole universe in sight of His moral creation. What is right will remain and what stenches of sin He will remove. His love for truth and justice will only be completed when He deals with injustice and sin through His revenge and wrath.

He who gave His son to uphold the honor of His word will judge all those who choose a lesser value than His greater worth. Abraham understood the impending severity of God's judgment. He said of Sodom:

"Far be it from Thee to do such a thing, to slay the righteous with the wicked, so that the righteous and the wicked are treated alike. Far be it from Thee! Shall not the Judge of all the earth deal justly?"[198]

"O let the evil of the wicked come to an end, but establish the righteous; for the righteous God tries the hearts and minds."[199]

"For the Lord loves justice, and does not forsake His godly ones; they are preserved forever; but the descendants of the wicked will be cut off."[200]

"He who justifies the wicked, and He who condemns the righteous, both of them are an abomination to the Lord."[201]

"And they said, 'Cornelius, a centurion, a righteous and God-fearing man well spoken of by the entire nation of the Jews, was divinely directed by a holy angel to send for you...'"[202]

God will not be unjust, and He will demand justice when He judges us one day. We should beware of that day and walk in a fear of the Lord every moment of our earthly lives.

Wrath of God

If God is loving and full of mercy, than how is it that He can get wrathful? If righteousness and justice are the foundation of His throne, than how is it that He can get wrathful? Often we will read about Old Testament characters and Psalmists pleading with God to restrain and stay His anger, and not to arouse His wrath.[203] And then how do we explain Jesus' anger in the temple when he turned over all the booths, and whipped the merchants and money-changers out of the synagogue? Had Jesus lost his patience, or was He a hypocrite who showed no love in anger?

These are all legitimate queries, but we must also acknowledge that these queries are projected from our finite, fallen minds, and our inherent mistrust of God's nature and character. First we must believe that if God is Love, than all his characteristics arise from Love. Thus if he ever gets angry or exhibits wrath, it will be due to injustice, unrighteousness, sin or any action or attitude that leads away from love and towards death. Imagine a doctor that gave no concern for a cancer that was destroying those He loved. Sin is like a cancer that God will remove. He is very clear that He becomes angry if we choose that of lesser value over God's great value. He is good and would do nothing from a malignant design, He is also great so He sees *more* injustice, perversion, and sin than our limited perception ever can.

God was willing to lay down His life to uphold integrity. He will therefore become angry at people who suppress the truth and willfully disregard His context.

"God is a righteous judge, and a God who has indignation every day."[204]

God's mercy, provided through the blood of the Lamb, will cover our sins. But do not be fooled; if we do not receive his grace, we will see the full wrath of God:

"...and they said to the mountains and to the rocks, 'Fall on us and hide us from the presence of Him who sits on the throne, and from the wrath of the Lamb."205

God is a shelter and a stronghold in times of trouble,[206] but if we do not fear Him or give Him the reverence that is due, we won't be safe with Him. It would be a terrifying reality to face the wrathful presence of the living God.

Chapter Twelve

Final Thoughts

God longs to give us what is best. You can hear His heart for us when He says:

"Oh that they had such a heart in them, that they would fear Me, and keep all My commandments always, that it may be well with them and with their sons forever!"[207]

God knows what is best for us and wants us to walk in the fullness of His beautiful design as released through our destiny. He is not a detached deity who wants to humiliate us because He enjoys watching us grovel. But our obedience to Him is crucial, because we must follow His commandments in order to understand His greatness and goodness better. The reality is we don't want what is best for us or for God. He is not limited and knows all that is going on. When we curse a deaf man, He hears it. When we place a stumbling block before the blind, He sees it. When we don't pay wages to hired workers, the first day, He is aware of it. He knows each thought as it passes through our mind, He sees each attitude as it is birthed and embraced by our will.

Let us be a people who love reality and walk in the truth. I recently tried to call my dad on my cell phone and for some reason, I didn't get through to him. I put the phone in my pocket while I spoke with another friend for a while. Later, I finally got a hold of my dad and he said, "You didn't turn your phone off, I could hear the whole conversation." My first reaction was fear. What did I say, I thought? I quickly realized that I had not said anything offensive or inflammatory. This is what I learned from this experience. If I was this vigilant regarding a simple, daily conversation with a friend, how much more vigilant should I be knowing that God is aware of everything I say, do, think, and everything in between. God will bring everything into account, and in the light of who He is and what He cares so strongly about, this is no small thing.

Pulitzer Prize author Annie Dillard describes our condition:

"Why do people in churches seem like cheerful, brainless tourists on a packaged tour of the absolute? On the whole I do not find Christians outside the catacombs sufficiently sensible of conditions. Does anyone have the foggiest idea what sort of power we so blithely invoke?

"Or, as I suspect, does no one believe a word of it? It is madness to wear velvet hats to church; we should all be wearing crash helmets, ushers should issue life preservers and signal flares. They should lash us to our pews. For the sleeping God may wake someday and take offence, or the waking God may draw us out to where we can never return."[208]

Let us be a people who live before the face of God in reverence and awe knowing that our God is who He says He is and will do what He says He will do. Let us remind ourselves that it is a terrifying thing to fall into the hands of a living God. He is a consuming fire and we will one day be before him. That, and that alone can set a 'context' for our life.

Join me in asking God for something so rare and precious that once gained, has the power to change my life and the life of those around me.

Father,
I need to know you in a new way. Not as my culture or family portrays you, a God of convenience and comfort, easily controlled and manipulated so that I can get what I want. Teach me to see you with eyes that discover the reality of who you are and in that sight, to be forever changed. To represent you as you are before a world that does not know you is the desire of my heart.
Thank you that your word says that if I ask for this, you will give it to me.
I stand in awe of you and love you.
In Jesus name.
Amen

Footnotes

Chapter One

[1] Genesis 20:2
[2] Genesis 20:11
[3] Hebrews 11:7
[4] I Samuel 17:26
[5] 1 Samuel 17:45
[6] Genesis 22:12
[7] Proverbs 3:25
[8] I John 4:18a
[9] I John 4:18b
[10] Kant, Immanuel. "Anthropology from a Pragmatic Viewpoint."
[11] Updike, John. "Self-Consciousness," *Memoirs*. 1989. Chapter 6.
[12] Emerson, Ralph Waldo. "Heroism," *Essays*. First Series, 1841.

Chapter Two

[13] Mark 12:28
[14] Mark 12:29
[15] Mark 12:30
[16] Deuteronomy 9:25-28
[17] Hebrews 11:6
[18] Acts 9:31
[19] Psalm 5:7
[20] Psalm 62:11-12
[21] Romans 1:20-22
[22] Isaiah 29:15
[23] Ezekiel 9:9
[24] Psalm 10:3-4
[25] Psalm 145:3

Chapter Three

[26] Deuteronomy 29:29
[27] Carlyle, Thomas. *Sartor Resartus*. Book 2, Chapter 9. 1833-1834.

[28] Faber, Frederick William. *The Right Must Win*
[29] Romans 12:33
[30] Proverbs 25:1
[31] Isaiah 44:6
[32] Psalm 90:2
[33] Isaiah 40:22
[34] Isaiah 40:25-26
[35] Emerson, Ralph Waldo. 1836 *Nature*, Chapter 1.
[36] Isaiah 40:12
[37] Jeremiah 10:7

Chapter Four

[38] Psalm 8:4-5
[39] Tozer, A.W. 1961, *The Knowlege of the Holy*, Harper, New York.
[40] Job 28:23-28
[41] Proverbs 9:10
[42] Andrew Murray, 1982, *Humility*, Whitaker house, pg. 10
[43] Isaiah 44:6
[44] Isaiah 44:8
[45] Isaiah 45:18
[46] Genesis 1:1
[47] Psalm 90:2
[48] Colossians 1:16-17
[49] Matthew 13:44-46
[50] Philippians 3:7-8
[51] Psalm 29:1-2
[52] Psalm 4:2
[53] Psalm 106:20
[54] Jeremiah 2:11
[55] Jeremiah 2:5
[56] Philippians 3:18-19
[57] Revelation 4:11, 5:9
[58] Psalm 101:3

Chapter Five

[59] Sterling, Bruce. "Peace is War," *Wired Magazine*. 10.04, April 2002.

[60] *MacMillan Contemporary Dictionary.* 1979, MacMillan Publishing Co., Inc., New York. Page 218
[61] John 3:19

Chapter Six

[62] Genesis 4:9
[63] Genesis 18:12
[64] Genesis 16
[65] Genesis 25:27-34
[66] Genesis 27
[67] Genesis 37
[68] Exodus 5
[69] Joshua 9
[70] James 1:5
[71] Matthew 6:24
[72] I John 2:16
[73] Barclay, W. 1960, *The Mind of Jesus.* London: SCM Press Limited. Pg s 159-161.
[74] II Chronicles 20:6
[75] II Chronicles 20:12
[76] II Chronicles 20:15-17
[77] Proverbs 1:7
[78] Ecclesiastes 3:1-8
[79] Ecclesiastes 12:13

Chapter Seven

[80] II Corinthians 2:14
[81] James 2:17

Chapter Eight

[82] John 14:34-35
[83] Manning, Brendan. 1990, *The Ragamuffin Gospel.* Multnomah Books: Oregon. Pg 121.
[84] Lewis, C.S. 1965, *The Weight of Glory,* Macmillan Publishing Co. New York,
[85] Lewis, C.S. 1965, *The Weight of Glory,* Macmillan Publishing Co. New York,
[86] Proverbs 25:11
[87] Genesis 2:7
[88] Genesis 3:19-20a

[89] James 3:8
[90] Proverbs 10:11
[91] James 1:26
[92] James 3:6
[93] James 3:2
[94] Matthew 12:34-36
[95] Proverbs 6:17
[96] I Thessalonians 5:18
[97] II Corinthians 11:23-27
[98] II Corinthians 4:17
[99] Romans 8:28
[100] Philippians 4:4
[101] Hebrews 12:28-29
[102] Hebrews 2:17-18
[103] I John 4:4
[104] I John 5:4
[105] John 8:44; Ephesians 6:6
[106] Romans 14:23
[107] I Corinthians 10:24-27
[108] Proverbs 2:1-3
[109] Proverbs 2:4-5
[110] Proverbs 1:29
[111] Lewis, C.S. 1988, *Mere Christianity*. Collins; Great Britain. Font Paperbacks
[112] Deuteronomy 30:19
[113] Galatians 6:4
[114] I Corinthians 13:12
[115] Proverbs 3:12
[116] Proverbs 15:33
[117] Philippians 4:8
[118] II Samuel 23:3-4
[119] Hebrews 11:6
[120] Matthew 8:9
[121] Matthew 8:10
[122] John 19:10-11
[123] Romans 13:1
[124] Isaiah 57:15
[125] Isaiah 66:2
[126] I Corinthians 13:1

[127] Psalm 25:15
[128] Psalm 123:2
[129] Matthew 28:19
[130] I Timothy 6:1
[131] Colossians 3:22-25
[132] Ephesians 5:22-25
[133] Exodus 20:12
[134] I Timothy 3:4
[135] I Timothy 5:8
[136] Proverbs 5:21
[137] Proverbs 4:23
[138] Psalm 44:21
[139] Proverbs 21:2
[140] Jeremiah 17:9-10
[141] I Samuel 16:7
[142] Psalm 51:10
[143] Psalm 51:17
[144] Psalm 7:9
[145] II Chronicles 16:9
[146] John 1:1
[147] Isaiah 11:2-3
[148] Proverbs 19:23
[149] Proverbs 16:6

Chapter Nine

[150] Romans 12:2
[151] Galatians 6:14
[152] Colossians 2:8
[153] James 1:27
[154] I John 2:15
[155] Joshua 24:15
[156] Joshua 23:8
[157] John 5:41-44
[158] Jeremiah 9:23-24
[159] I Samuel 15:24-26
[160] I Samuel 15:27-30
[161] Ecclesiastes 1:2
[162] Isaiah 51:12-13
[163] Luke 16:15
[164] Matthew 6:5

[165] Matthew 23:5
[166] Matthew 23:27
[167] Isaiah 29:13
[168] Psalm 133:1-3, John 15:12, John 17:21, Romans 12:10, I John 4:7
[169] Deuteronomy 4:24
[170] Lewis, C.S. 1988, *Mere Christianity*. Collins; Great Britain. Font Paperbacks
[171] Psalm 10:4
[172] Lewis, C.S. 1988, *Mere Christianity*. Collins; Great Britain. Font Paperbacks
[173] Ezekiel 28:7, Obadiah 1:3, Jeremiah 49:16, Isaiah 2:12
[174] Proverbs 16:5

Chapter Ten

[175] James 4:6
[176] Bowler, T. Downing. *General Systems Thinking* – its scope and applicability. Series Volume 4. North Holland, New York, Oxford.
[177] II Kings 17:33
[178] James 2:19

Chapter Eleven

[179] I John 4:8
[180] Romans 5:8
[181] Romans 8:35-39
[182] Romans 14:7-8
[183] Psalm 103:11
[184] Psalm 118:4
[185] Psalm 33:18, Psalm 147:11
[186] Romans 10:3
[187] Romans 1:16-17
[188] Isaiah 51:7
[189] Malachi 4:2
[190] Acts 10:35
[191] Revelation 15:4
[192] II Corinthians 7:1
[193] Ezekiel 36:23
[194] Hebrews 12:10

[195] Psalm 113:4-6
[196] Proverbs 22:4
[197] Luke 1:50
[198] Genesis 18:25
[199] Psalm 7:9
[200] Psalm 37:28
[201] Proverbs 17:15
[202] Acts 10:22
[203] Psalm 78:38
[204] Psalm 7:11
[205] Revelations 6:16
[206] Psalm 9:9

Chapter Twelve

[207] Deuteronomy 5:29
[208] Parish, Fawn. 1999, *Honor: What love looks like*, Regal books.

About the Author

Matt Rawlins works with the Youth With A Mission / University of the Nations as a teacher and travels internationally as a trainer and consultant dealing with leadership and organizational issues.

With a Ph. D. in Philosophy, Matt has a heart to see people understand who they are and specifically, to help leaders communicate about difficult issues in times of change.

The author of nine books, Matt is a gifted writer and communicator.

After living in Asia for ten years, he now resides with his wife Celia and son Joshua in Kailua-Kona, Hawaii.

You can contact him at:

mrawlins@hawaii.rr.com

CPSIA information can be obtained
at www.ICGtesting.com
Printed in the USA
LVOW03s2355051017
551392LV00001B/41/P